D0560944

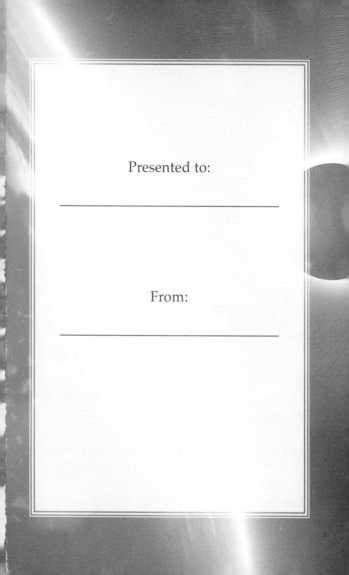

Presented to:

_____

From:

_____

with Dr. David Jeremiah

© 2001, 2008, 2017 by Turning Point for God

P.O. Box 3838

San Diego, CA 92163

All Rights Reserved

Unless otherwise indicated, Scripture verses are quoted from the NEW KING JAMES VERSION.

Printed in the United States of America.

Answers to
Questions About
PROPHECY

DAVID JEREMIAH

Table of Contents

Act 4
The Millennium   **105**

ACT 5
The New Heaven and the New Earth 117

Watch therefore, for you do not know what hour your Lord is coming.

~ Matthew 24:42

INTRODUCTION

The study of End Times can cause questions, apprehension, and fear. People often comment: "Why do I need to study prophecy?" "It is too complicated." "I don't understand what it means." Or some even express that the study of prophecy makes them anxious and nervous. I will not argue with the fact that studying prophecy can be complex and overwhelming. It is difficult to see how these obscure passages can have any significance for me today. They appear to lack relevance to what we are going through right now.

If we continue with this mindset, we will miss the rich truth God has provided for us. We cannot understand where we are now if we don't understand where we are going. To help you gain an understanding and appreciation for this difficult topic, I have compiled this book with your most frequently asked questions about biblical prophecy. In order to answer these puzzling and debatable questions, I have opened the Scriptures as my one and only source.

I encourage you to study God's plan for the future. What you believe about many of these issues can determine what side you are on when God decides to draw the final curtain on the drama of history. I am confident you will find, as I have, that studying and understanding the events of tomorrow will change your view of today!

Awaiting His return,

David Jeremiah

DAVID JEREMIAH

ACT 1

The Rapture

To Take His Church Home

Christ's coming is fast approaching. It seems that all the prophecies which must be completed before His return have been fulfilled. The Lord will descend with a shout and the trumpet of God. All believers, living and dead, will suddenly meet the Lord in the air. Like an eager bride, the Church waits for the final culmination of the union with her Groom.

Excerpt from
Until Christ Returns:

As bad as it is today in our world, it could (and will) get worse. A restraining influence in our world holds this evil—this dark satanic tide of perversion and lawlessness—in check. Who has the power to restrain Satan? Only God. And it is God the Holy Spirit, the third person of the Trinity, who draws the line today and keeps the ocean of evil at bay.

(Chapter 3, "Do Not Be Troubled," page 57)

What signs indicate that the End Times are near?

The Sign of Deception

Many people are going to claim to be the Messiah and claim to have the answers for a troubled world. Jesus says to "take heed"—literally, to keep our eyes open so we are not fooled. In the End Times, people will be crying desperately for leaders to deliver them, and they will seek mystics and religious leaders who claim to have deeper knowledge.

The Sign of Disputes Among Nations

As wars and dissension among groups of people begin to escalate, we know it is a sign of Christ's return. The book of Revelation tells us that the Tribulation period is filled with war—ceaseless, unending, terrible war—that will escalate until the entire world is involved. Fifty percent of all research scientists today are involved in arms development. Despite all the arms limitations treaties, there is at least one military weapon and 4,000 pounds of explosives for every man, woman, and child on earth. The Bible says that as we move toward the End Times, there will be constant talk of conflicts, border skirmishes, race wars, and national battles.

The Sign of Devastation

Today, as you read this, millions of people in the world are going hungry, even though God has blessed us with a fruitful, abundant planet. As we get closer to the End Times, there will be more and more famine. There will also be earthquakes, something that science has said will happen. Christ also spoke of pestilence: the spread of new diseases. Our world is experiencing a spate of tragic new diseases that we are unable to control.

The Sign of Deliverance Into the Tribulation

Just before Jesus returns, there will be an explosion of antagonism toward God's people. Christians will be persecuted. I think we are already seeing it. The media holds most fringe groups in high regard, but it seems to attack conservative Christians every chance it gets. Many are going to pay a high price for living out their faith in our world.

As Christians, how should we prepare for the approaching End Times?

Stand Fast (2 Thessalonians 2:15)

This is not a time to go running after new doctrine. This is not the time to be exploring new ideas about theology. Stand fast in the truth that you know. If there has ever been a time for us to be unequivocal about our truth, this is it. The buzzword today is "tolerance." But I want to be only as tolerant as God is, and God is quite *intolerant* of what is not true.

Hold On (2 Thessalonians 2:15)

The daily news can discourage us. But in the midst of it all, there is Jesus and His encouragement. We need to cultivate our relationship with Him until He is not just one of the things in our life, but He is the one thing in our life—the focus of who we are.

Work Hard (2 Thessalonians 2:16-17; Luke 19:13, KJV)

The objective is not only to go to heaven, but to take as many people with us as we can. Share the Gospel, teach children, build one another up, strengthen one another, encourage those who are fallen, and reach out to those who are hurting. In every good work, "Occupy till I come," said the Lord. This is no time for idleness. This is a time for us to seek the truth and live it out every day.

EXCERPT FROM
WHAT IN THE WORLD IS GOING ON?:

In spite of the high value I place on understanding future events, I find that studying prophecy has an even higher and more practical value. It provides a compelling motivation for living the Christian life. The immediacy of prophetic events shows the need to live each moment in Christlike readiness.

(Chapter 10, "The Return of the King," page 232)

What is the difference between the Rapture and the Second Coming of Christ?

The Rapture:

The Church, including the dead in Christ and those who are alive in Christ, meets with Christ in the air (1 Thessalonians 4:13-5:10; Philippians 3:20-21; Colossians 3:4; 1 Peter 1:3-7; Titus 2:11-13). "Then we who are alive *and* remain shall be caught up together with them in the clouds to meet the Lord in the air. And thus we shall always be with the Lord" (1 Thessalonians 4:17). The Rapture of the Church takes place between Revelation chapters 3 and 4. Christ raptures His Church up into heaven before the Tribulation to remove the Christians from the coming judgment on the earth.

The Second Coming:

Jesus comes in power and great glory at the end of the Tribulation. He will come in judgment and will reign on this earth during the Millennium. At this time, everyone will know He is King. "Immediately after the tribulation of those days the sun will be darkened, and the moon will not give its light; the stars will fall from heaven, and the powers of the heavens will be shaken. Then the sign of the Son of Man will appear in heaven, and then all the tribes of the earth will mourn, and they will see the Son of Man coming on the clouds of heaven with power and great glory. And He will send His angels with a great sound of a trumpet, and they will gather together His elect from the four winds, from one end of heaven to the other" (Matthew 24:29-31).

Christ's First Appearance

Tribulation

Christ's Second Appearance

The Judgment
of all who rejected Him

Christ will return not only to reward His own, but to judge the world. Between His first appearance and His second, will be a time of trouble, and then will occur the judgment of all those who rejected Him. This will not be a judgment for believers, for they have already stood before the Judgment Seat. This will be a judgment with no parole, no lenient sentence, and no pleas of insanity.

(Chapter 1, "Warnings Ignored," page 27)

What events will take place in heaven after the Rapture?

After the Rapture, we will come before the Judgment Seat of Christ one by one. The Judgment Seat is not about whether we will enter heaven—we'll already be there. It will be a time to give an account of the works we have done on earth, and we will be rewarded accordingly. We'll be assigned places of authority in the coming Millennium based upon our faithfulness to God when we were on earth, as well as the influence we left behind.

> *For we must all appear before the judgment seat of Christ, that each one may receive the things done in the body, according to what he has done, whether good or bad.*
> *~ 2 Corinthians 5:10*

Will I be a part of the Rapture if my body has been cremated?

When the Scripture says, "The dead in Christ will rise," it is speaking of the bodily resurrection of believers. At this time, the spirits of believers will be united with their perfect and complete resurrection bodies. "For the Lord Himself will descend from heaven with a shout, with the voice of an archangel, and with the trumpet of God. And the dead in Christ will rise first. Then we who are alive *and* remain shall be caught up together with them in the clouds to meet the Lord in the air. And thus we shall always be with the Lord. Therefore comfort one another with these words" (1 Thessalonians 4:16-18).

Why should I avoid determining a date and time for the Rapture?

The fact is, we cannot calculate the day Christ will return because God specifically chose not to reveal it to us.

When the apostles asked Jesus about apocalyptic time, He replied gently but firmly, "It is not for you to know times or seasons which the Father has put in His own authority. But you shall receive power when the Holy Spirit has come upon you ..." (Acts 1:7-8). Only God knows what time it is, and only God knows when these times will run out. God's calendar is the only one that matters (1 Thessalonians 5:1-2; Matthew 24:36, 42, 44, 50; 25:13).

Future truth impacts present responsibility. It is the knowledge that His coming is soon that puts a little bit of urgency into our step and a little bit of determination into our service.

ACT 2

The Tribulation

To Allow Unrestrained Evil

The moment after the Rapture, the Spirit of God will remove any restraining influence on earth. As a result, life on earth will be relinquished to flourishing evil. As the Tribulation progresses, evil will result in a climax of worsening conditions. God's wrath will be displayed toward the wicked through the signs of His coming judgment. Thankfully, those who are believers at the time of the Rapture will be spared from this terrible time.

EXCERPT FROM
ESCAPE THE COMING NIGHT:

The hour-hand on God's timeclock is wound up and spinning. We are being swept along the path of history by a swift wind at our backs. Our individual ability to weather the storm will come from our understanding of the Word of God. We need only heed what has echoed through the centuries: "He who has an ear, let him hear what the Spirit says to the churches" (Revelation 3:22).

(Chapter 5, "The Lukewarm Church in the Last Days," page 82)

What signs will warn of the approaching Tribulation period?

These ten events are the things we can expect in embryonic form in the days preceding the Rapture and the beginning of the Tribulation. These ten things will continue to multiply and progress as the first three and one-half years of the Great Tribulation unfold.

A Time of Deception

"Many will come in My name, saying, 'I am the Christ,' and will deceive many" (Matthew 24:5).

A Time of Dissension

"... you will hear of wars and rumors of wars .... Nation will rise against nation, and kingdom against kingdom ..." (Matthew 24:6-7).

A Time of Devastation

"… there will be famines …" (Matthew 24:7).

A Time of Disease

" … pestilences …" (Matthew 24:7).

A Time of Disasters

" … and earthquakes in various places" (Matthew 24:7).

A Time of Death

"They will deliver you up to tribulation and kill you, and you will be hated by all nations for My name's sake" (Matthew 24:9).

A Time of Disloyalty

"And then many will be offended, will betray one another, and will hate one another" (Matthew 24:10).

A Time of Delusion

"Then many false prophets will rise up and deceive many" (Matthew 24:11). It should also be noted that part of the delusion will be an increase in drug use. One of the characteristics of the End Times' false religion will be what the book of Revelation calls "sorceries" (9:21). The word John uses is *pharmakia*, from which we get the word *pharmacy*. It is an ancient reference to the ingestion of drugs. The use of mind-altering substances such as narcotics and hallucinogens will be associated with false religions, doubtless with the approval of the government.

A Time of Defection

"And because lawlessness will abound, the love of many will grow cold" (Matthew 24:12). People will turn away from God and from each other.

A Time of Declaration

"And this gospel of the kingdom will be preached in all the world as a witness to all the nations ..." (Matthew 24:14).

"The false prophet will be allowed to spread evil during the Tribulation, but God is merely biding His time. One day God's justice will prevail, and the false prophet will meet his fiery end ... He will be 'cast alive into the lake of fire.'"

Agents of the Apocalypse, chapter 7, "The Beast From the Earth," pages 180-181.

What will happen on earth during the Tribulation?

The moment after the Rapture, the Spirit of God will remove any restraining influence on earth so that things will be far, far worse even than today. This is a seven-year period described in Revelation 11-18. After the first three and one-half years of that time, there will be the climax of worsening conditions, the anger of God against the wicked, and the signs of Christ's coming. During the last three and one-half years, the "lawless one"— the Antichrist—will be empowered to sit at the center of the Tribulation's evil as he personifies Satan.

The Creator of the earth is worshiped by the Church in heaven.

What will happen in heaven during the Tribulation?

The Christians are in heaven. God is seated on the throne, which is surrounded by a rainbow of emerald greens. The 24 elders representing the church-age saints sit around the throne. Before the throne is a sea of glass. In the midst of the throne are the four living creatures, and singing praise to the throne are the angels and the Church. This is the worship of the glorified Christ, the Creator of the world. God is just about to deal with the physical earth in judgment, and before He does, the Creator of earth is worshiped by the Church in heaven. Thunder, lightning, and voices signify the judgment which is about to fall on the earth.

Will Christians escape the Tribulation?

Christians will escape the seven-year nightmare of the Tribulation.

I believe the Bible clearly teaches that one of the coming great events in the fulfillment of prophecy concerns the Church. This is the personal, bodily return of the Lord to remove from earth His waiting Church and to reward them according to their works. This will take place before the Tribulation period during which time the judgments of God will be poured out upon the unbelieving world.

I believe there are more Scriptures to support the imminent return of Christ for His Church prior to the Tribulation than during or after it: 1 Thessalonians 4:13-18; 2 Thessalonians 2:8-12; Matthew 24:29-31; Revelation 3:10.

"Those who are wise will shine like the brightness of the heavens, and those who lead many to righteousness, like the stars forever and ever" (Daniel 12:3, NIV). In the midst of all the difficult times, the horror of the Tribulation, God has some special things that He has reserved for those who serve Him. He says they are to become like stars in His galaxy!

(Chapter 20, "The End Times," page 240)

What natural disasters will occur on earth during the Tribulation?

The sun will turn black, the moon will turn red, and great earthquakes will be common.

Revelation 6:12 says, "… behold, there was a great earthquake …." It also says, "… the sun became black as sackcloth of hair, and the moon became like blood." When Jesus died on the cross, the whole earth became dark at midday. When Egypt was judged, there was a blackness of night. When the Lord came down at Mt. Sinai, the mountain was shrouded in black clouds. The prophets, as well, said darkness would occur at the beginning of the Tribulation period.

The stars will fall out of the sky.

"And the stars of heaven fell to the earth …" (Revelation 6:13). The word "star" here is the Greek word *aster* and it refers to luminous bodies in the sky other than the sun and moon. Clearly these stars are not the distant stellar objects we know as stars but more like a group of asteroids.

The mountains and islands will move.

"… every mountain and island was moved out of its place" (Revelation 6:14). When the asteroids hit the earth, the possibility is that the earth's crust will be so disturbed by the impact that great segments of it will actually begin to slip and slide over the earth's mantle. According to Dr. Henry Morris, those living in the regions above such shifting will observe the heavens appearing to move in the opposite direction, as if they are being "rolled up."

The ocean will become blood.

As Revelation 8:8-9 explains, a great mountain burning with fire is cast into the sea. The sea will become blood and one-third of all sea life will die. There will also be the destruction of one-third of all the ships. The far-reaching implications of these judgments are beyond our understanding. Someone has reasoned that the oceans occupy about three-fourths of the earth's surface, so the extent of this judgment will be staggering. The pollution of the water and the death of so many sea creatures will vastly affect the balance of life in the ocean. This will happen to one-third of the saltwater bodies of the world.

The water will become poisoned.

The freshwater supplies will be affected. They become bitter, with the result that many people will die (Revelation 8:10-11). The instrument of judgment will be a great star that is labeled "Wormwood." This literal star or meteor hurtling through space will approach the earth. Sweeping along the surface of the earth, it will turn one-third of the water of the earth into a deadly poisonous liquid. It will affect the rivers, springs, and wells.

The condition of the Gospel going to the whole world is a condition not of the Rapture, but of the Second Coming of Christ.

> **The entire world will hear the Gospel before Christ returns. Jesus could come at any time. How can both of these statements be true?**

He could come tonight! You may hear people say that the Rapture cannot occur until the whole world has heard the Gospel; therefore, we need to preach the Gospel to every creature so that the last person to be saved is brought into the kingdom, at which time Jesus will return for His Church. This cannot be true.

If there is anything that has yet to happen before Christ's return, there is no such thing as the imminent return of Jesus Christ. The command to take the Gospel into the whole world is certainly pressing upon every generation, but the condition of the Gospel going to the whole world is a condition not of the Rapture, but of the Second Coming of Christ.

Will people be saved during the Tribulation?

Yes, there will be a great harvest of souls for Christ during the Tribulation. In this harvest of souls, we see fulfilled the prophecy contained in Matthew 24:14—"And this gospel of the kingdom will be preached in all the world as a witness to all the nations, and then the end will come."

People from every nation, tribe, and language will be part of the great redeemed multitude. This is going to be a time of the greatest suffering and persecution the world has ever seen, and it will also be a time when the greatest wave of genuine conversion ever takes place. This multitude of redeemed ones will come from those who were still unsaved at the time of the Rapture.

Today there are at least two billion people who have never heard or understood enough of the Gospel to accept or reject it. Those who will be saved during the Tribulation will come from this great number. Those who are saved during the Tribulation will be saved on exactly the same basis as those before the Tribulation, which is by the death and justifying resurrection of the Son of God.

There will be a great harvest of souls during the Tribulation.

How will people be saved during the Tribulation?

If there are no believers on earth at the beginning of the seven years of the Tribulation, this is a good question. As we will discuss in upcoming pages, there will be Two Witnesses and 144,000 sealed Israelites. In addition, Dr. Henry Morris suggests a "silent witness" because "millions upon millions of copies of the Bible and Bible portions ... will not [be] remove[d] and multitudes will no doubt be constrained to read the Bible in those days ... [and] will turn to their Creator and Savior." These blood-bought believers will begin to warn others of even more severe judgment to come. They will preach repentance and judgment and they will be killed for their message.

If someone becomes a Christian during the Tribulation, what will happen to them when they die?

The Lord sends an angel for their own special blessing: Blessed are the dead who die in the Lord (Revelation 14:13). Just as the New Testament begins with the Beatitudes of Jesus for the living, it ends with the Beatitude of Jesus for the dying. This is the second of the seven Beatitudes found in the book of Revelation. Even though these words are particularly written for those who die during the Tribulation, they are also written for the saints of every generation. For the dead in Christ of all ages. The believer does not die in the sense of death being the end; he is simply waiting for the coming of the Lord. Blessed are those who have gone to sleep in Jesus.

If I can be saved during the Tribulation, why should I change my life now?

Just as death terminates the day of possible salvation for those who reject Christ, so does the Rapture. Those who have heard the Gospel message and have rejected it will be given a "strong delusion" during the Tribulation. Second Thessalonians 2:10-11 tells us, "… because they did not receive the love of the truth, that they might be saved. And for this reason God will send them strong delusion, that they should believe the lie …." Revelation 13 tells us it will be the lies of the Beast and the Antichrist, who fabricate the life of Christ and bring deception. Believing these deceptions, the people who have rejected the Gospel before the Tribulation will go to hell. The day of grace will be over for them. There is no second chance.

Be warned: You had better not wait to become a Christian. I've heard people reason like this before, but I have to wonder about someone's legitimate desire to know God if it is coupled with a desire to beat the system. Do not let anyone tell you that you can beat the system by waiting until the Tribulation to become a Christian. It won't happen. You'll be deceived. The reason more people aren't saved today is because of deception. It's amazing, but the more the Tribulation grows in intensity, the more people reject God. You'd think they would turn to Him and cry for mercy, but instead they curse Him who sends judgment on the earth. Those who reject the truth now will be deceived and will never believe the Gospel when they hear it preached.

The Bible says today is the day of salvation (2 Corinthians 6:2). Don't try to get around God's plan. Don't think you can beat the system. One day soon the Lord is coming back, and if you have already rejected Him, the day of opportunity will be gone.

Behold, now is the accepted time; behold, now is the day of salvation.
~ 2 Corinthians 6:2

Is it true that it will be impossible for someone to kill themselves during the Tribulation?

Yes, even though men will seek to die and suicide will be attempted, apparently death will not be possible: "In those days men will seek death and will not find it; they will desire to die, and death will flee from them" (Revelation 9:6).

It will be such an awful experience for those who are left to endure the result of countless demons from the pit running unchecked throughout the earth. The only people these demons are allowed to sting are those who do not belong to God (verse 4). The poison from the sting will set the nerve center on fire (verse 10). This evil will be stretched out for 150 days (verse 10) and death cannot provide escape (verse 6).

Will promiscuity be prevalent on earth during the Tribulation?

When divine restraint is withdrawn during the Tribulation, human passions will break loose and morality will be discarded in favor of licentiousness and sexual immorality. The result will be nothing less than rampant promiscuity.

> *Blessed are those who do His commandments, that they may have the right to the tree of life, and may enter through the gates into the city. But outside are dogs and sorcerers and sexually immoral and murderers and idolaters, and whoever loves and practices a lie.*
> *~ Revelation 22:14-15*

Who are the Two Witnesses that will preach the Gospel during the Tribulation?

I believe one witness to be Elijah the prophet, reincarnated. In Malachi 3:1-3 and 4:5-6 we are told that Elijah will come before Jesus returns. This prophecy is fulfilled in Revelation 11. Another reason I believe it to be Elijah is because Elijah didn't die. Elijah was taken to heaven in a whirlwind of fire. Elijah also uses the same sign in the Tribulation as he used when he was a prophet. In 1 Kings 17, Elijah stopped the rain; in Revelation 11:6, he is seen to "have power to shut heaven, so that no rain falls in the days of their prophecy ...." It is also significant that Elijah appeared with Moses in the Transfiguration.

Who is the second witness? I believe it to be Moses for these reasons: Moses and Elijah had already been paired together at the

Transfiguration. Moses performed the second half of the miracles where we see Elijah performing the first. For example, Elijah shut heaven and Moses turned waters to blood. Moses died, but no one knows where his body is buried (Deuteronomy 34:5-6). The body of Moses was preserved by God so that he might be restored. In the Jewish culture, the Law and the prophets are understood. Moses is the Law, and Elijah is the prophet.

It is impossible to prove conclusively who these Two Witnesses are. But, if they are not these two men, we can know they are very much like them and have the same kind of ministry.

When will these witnesses appear?

In Revelation 11:3, we are introduced to the Two Witnesses. There is much debate as to when these witnesses appear on the scene. I believe they begin their ministry at the beginning of the Tribulation, when the Antichrist makes his covenant with the Jewish people. We can assume they will have a great following.

> *"And I will give power to my two witnesses, and they will prophesy one thousand two hundred and sixty days, clothed in sackcloth."* *These are the two olive trees and the two lampstands standing before the God of the earth.*
> ~ *Revelation 11:3-4*

What special powers will the Two Witnesses possess?

Revelation 11:5 says, "And if anyone wants to harm them, fire proceeds from their mouth and devours their enemies." God has provided them with protection. These witnesses will have power over death, drought, and disease. They preach about Christ as Lord of all the earth. They shut the heavens so no rain can fall during their ministry, and they have power to cause plagues as often as they desire. They go about testifying of the wickedness of the people. They tell the people that God is responsible for all the judgments that have been poured out. If that is not enough, they will tell them of more terrifying judgments to come. They preach against the Beast of Revelation 13 and anger the Jews by telling them their worship in the temple is pure paganism. Men try to destroy them because their witness exposes the wickedness of the earth.

EXCERPT FROM
AGENTS OF THE APOCALYPSE:

In biblical times, God often used Two Witnesses to validate a truth. Two angels testified to the resurrection of the Savior. Two men in white testified to His ascension. God often dispatches His people in twos as well. Think of Moses and Aaron, Joshua and Caleb, Zerubbabel and Joshua, Peter and John, Paul and Silas, Timothy and Titus. The disciples were sent out two by two, and the seventy were also told to travel in pairs. These Two Witnesses will follow that pattern as they proclaim one of the most important calls to repentance of all time.

(Chapter 4, "The Two Witnesses," pages 95-96)

What will happen to these witnesses?

After 42 months, during which time they cannot be killed, the Two Witnesses will be killed by the Beast who ascends from the bottomless pit. The Two Witnesses are so hated that the entire world will rejoice at their deaths. Their bodies will be put on public display. Their bodies will lie in the street for three and one-half days. In biblical Jewish society this was an abomination. Their enemies will be ecstatic that someone has finally put an end to these two nemeses.

They are already decomposing, and the next action we see is that they stand up! The whole world will see this because they are looking in on the scene through the news and the papers. While they are the focus of world attention, they are not only resurrected, they are raptured (Revelation 11:12). They go up to heaven in "a cloud." This cloud is the *shekinah* glory of God. It is the same cloud that the angel of Revelation 10:1 was clothed in.

> *Now after the three-and-a-half days the breath of life from God entered them, and they stood on their feet, and great fear fell on those who saw them. And they heard a loud voice from heaven saying to them, "Come up here." And they ascended to heaven in a cloud, and their enemies saw them.*
>
> *~ Revelation 11:11-12*

If Satan was defeated at the Cross, why does he appear to be winning?

The ultimate victory has been won at Calvary, but it will be implemented in the future. The sentence has been passed, now it needs to be enforced. The enforcement is in the hands of the Church. The tool that enforces Satan's defeat is the tool of prayer. "For the weapons of our warfare *are* not carnal but mighty in God for pulling down strongholds, casting down arguments and every high thing that exalts itself against the knowledge of God, bringing every thought into captivity to the obedience of Christ" (2 Corinthians 10:4-5). One person praying on earth can move angels in heaven.

Christians need to learn the power of prayer against Satan, and that he will be defeated in his work. We are not engaged in the warfare if we are not praying against Satan. The judgment that was effected at the Cross, and is enforced through prayer, will be completed. Satan is doomed. But if we don't enforce that judgment in our own lives, we will be victims instead of victors.

> *And war broke out in heaven: Michael and his angels fought with the dragon; and the dragon and his angels fought, but they did not prevail, nor was a place found for them in heaven any longer. So the great dragon was cast out, that serpent of old, called the Devil and Satan, who deceives the whole world; he was cast to the earth, and his angels were cast out with him. Then I heard a loud voice saying in heaven, "Now salvation, and strength, and the kingdom of our God, and the power of His Christ have come, for the accuser of our brethren, who accused them before our God day and night, has been cast down."*
> *~ Revelation 12:7-10*

What is the "unholy trinity"?

Satan is the first person and the father of the unholy trinity. The Antichrist is the second person and the son of the unholy trinity. While the Holy Spirit is the third person of the Trinity and His main function is to direct praise to the person of Christ, the False Prophet's major function is to direct the worship and praise of the people back to the Antichrist (Revelation 13:11-12).

The Two Trinities		
Person	**Holy**	**Unholy**
First	Father	Satan
Second	Son	Antichrist
Third	Holy Spirit	False Prophet

Who is the Antichrist?

The Antichrist will be a charismatic leader who will be able to sway the masses with his speaking ability. Daniel 7 says that he will have "a mouth speaking pompous words" (verse 8). "He shall speak great words against the most High" (verse 25, KJV). "And he was given a mouth speaking great things and blasphemies …" (Revelation 13:5). The Antichrist will be noted in his career for wonderful eloquence, and will be able to capture the attention and admiration of the world. Because of his ability as an orator, he will stand in front of the world's people and galvanize them into a mighty force.

Daniel 7:20 describes the Antichrist as one "whose appearance *was* greater than his fellows." With his great magnetic personality, this man will cause people to flock to him. Daniel 7:8 says that, "… in this horn, *were* eyes like the eyes of a man ...." Verse 20 speaks of his eyes again. This refers to his mental ability, his intellect, his cleverness, his uncommon wisdom and cunning.

The Antichrist is represented as a Beast—an appropriate title for him (Revelation 13:1-10).

During the last three and one-half years of the Tribulation, the Antichrist will personify Satan himself. Second Thessalonians 2:9 says, "The coming of the *lawless one* is according to the working of Satan, with all power, signs, and lying wonders."

> *The Antichrist will be noted in his career for wonderful eloquence, and will be able to capture the attention and admiration of the world.*

How does the Antichrist gain political power?

His rise to power is inconspicuous. He will rise up out of the masses. John says, "Then I stood on the sand of the sea. And I saw a beast rising up out of the sea, having seven heads and ten horns …" (Revelation 13:1). Usually in the book of Revelation, when you see the word "sea," it has a reference to the rising up from the masses of people.

Whatever power the Antichrist has, he only has it by virtue of the fact that he is allowed to have it by God Almighty. As bad as the Tribulation is, it is never out of God's control. There is a leash on Satan, and God is holding on to the other end of the leash. Satan will be able to do only that which God allows him to do in the consummation of the end of the age.

EXCERPT FROM

WHAT IN THE WORLD IS GOING ON?:

The combination of magnetic personality, speaking ability, and extreme good looks will make him virtually irresistible to the masses. When he comes on the scene, people will flock to him like flies to honey, and they will fall over themselves to do anything he asks.

(Chapter 7, "When One Man Rules the World," page 148)

Who will worship the Antichrist?

According to Revelation 13:8, "All who dwell on the earth will worship him …." Daniel 7:25 tells us that the Antichrist is a cultic leader. "He shall speak *pompous* words against the Most High … and shall intend to change times and law." He will speak out against the true God of heaven. The language suggests that he will try to raise himself to the level of God and make declarations from that position.

Second Thessalonians 2:4 says of the Antichrist, "Who opposes and exalts himself above all that is called God or that is worshiped, so that he sits as God in the temple of God, showing himself that he is God." He will accept the worship of the peoples of the world.

There will be Christians on earth when the Antichrist is there, and the Bible says he will wear them out with persecutions. They will be martyred for their faith. (The believers of our present age will be in heaven.) The expression used for this wearing out is one of wearing out garments, a slow process. The program of the Antichrist will be one of property seizure, economic squeeze, mark of the Beast, torture, and murder.

> *The coming of the lawless one is according to the working of Satan, with all power, signs, and lying wonders.*
> *~ 2 Thessalonians 2:9*

What is the mark of the Beast?

The mark of the Beast is 666. We can't identify the exact significance of the mark, but there are some general things we can say about it: The number six is the number of man, as it says in Revelation 13:18. Man was created on the sixth day. He is to work six out of seven days. A Hebrew slave could not be a slave more than six years. The Jews' fields could not be sown for more than six years running.

Here is wisdom. Let him who has understanding calculate the number of the beast, for it is the number of a man: His number is 666.
~ Revelation 13:18

Perhaps the Beast in his number 666 represents the ultimate in human ingenuity and competence. The Antichrist is all about putting together man's last fling at ruling the world. He raises up this image, requiring it to be stamped on every human alive at that time.

The word used for the mark is the Greek word *charagma*. In antiquity, this word was always associated with the Roman Emperor. It often contained the Emperor's name, his effigy, and the year of his reign. It was necessary for buying and selling, and was required to be affixed to documents to attest to their validity.

"He causes all, both small and great, rich and poor, free and slave, to receive a mark on their right hand or on their foreheads, and that no one may buy or sell except one who has the mark or the name of the beast, or the number of his name" (Revelation 13:16-17).

What will happen to those who refuse the mark?

Those who refuse to receive the mark of the Beast will suffer the wrath of the Antichrist. But Revelation 19:19-21 warns that all who receive the mark of the Beast will suffer eternal judgment at the hand of God.

Babylon is God's name for the world's system of the Beast. Worship the Beast and be damned by God, or worship God and be damned by the Beast. According to the system organized by the Beast, if you don't wear his mark, you can't buy, sell, work, or function. The angel announces that if you do wear the mark of the Beast, you have consigned yourself to eternal fire, damnation, and separation from God. There is no in-between ground.

The torment of those who worship the Beast will last forever. The mark of the Beast indicates that the one wearing it is a worshiper of the Beast and submits to his rule. To be without the mark is to be labeled a traitor. The people who do not have the mark will be killed, or starved simply because they will not be able to get the food and other things they need to stay alive (Revelation 14:9-11).

> *The angel announces that if you do wear the mark of the Beast, you have consigned yourself to eternal fire, damnation, and separation from God.*

How will the Beast be defeated?

Satan allows the Beast to be killed, or at least to appear to be killed. But the head wound will be healed, and the world will be so astonished they will follow him. Once again the imitator is at work. He will feign the Resurrection. This is Satan's last fling. He will use everything at his disposal to take as many people to hell with him as he can.

Just when it seems there is no hope, when the bottom is finally reached and evil rules, the Second Coming will finally come about and God's Son will dethrone the Beast. Christ will intervene in the Battle of Armageddon, have victory, and the nations and Israel will now be judged. Christ will institute a new thousand-year rule, and the Millennium will begin.

Who is the False Prophet?

In reality the False Prophet is a Satan-possessed man who exercises authority and military power in the name of the Antichrist. He does miraculous things to cause the whole world to bow down and worship the Antichrist and his image. Jesus says in Matthew 7:15, "Beware of false prophets, who come to you in sheep's clothing, but inwardly they are ravenous wolves." The False Prophet in Revelation is the epitome of every false prophet who has gone before him. We need to be warned against false prophets who come with the voice and personality and calmness of a lamb, but who speak the words of Satan himself.

> *The False Prophet is a Satan-possessed man who exercises authority and military power in the name of the Antichrist.*

What will the False Prophet look like?

According to Revelation 13:11, he has the voice of a dragon, but he looks like a lamb. Why would Satan design the False Prophet to look like a lamb? He is continuing the counterfeiting ministry of doing everything he can to deceive people into thinking that the False Prophet lamb is the Lamb who was slain before the foundation of the world.

As a lamb, he will appear meek and mild—a counterfeit of the true gentleness of Jesus.

What powers will the False Prophet have?

The False Prophet will be the Antichrist's religious leader and will have the power to counterfeit the miracles of God according to Revelation 13:13. The specific miracle mentioned in the text is the calling down of fire from heaven. The False Prophet may be trying to imitate Elijah, when he called down fire on Mount Carmel, to make people think he *is* Elijah who is coming before the great and terrible day of the Lord. He deceives people into building an image as a central point of worship for the Beast. With his occultic powers, he will enable the image to speak.

Excerpt from
What in the World Is Going On?:

The Antichrist will aggressively live up to his terrible name. He will be Satan's Superman, who persecutes, tortures, and kills the people of God and leads the armies of the world into the climactic battle of Armageddon. He will be the most powerful dictator the world has ever seen, making Caesar, Hitler, Mao, and Saddam seem weak and tame by comparison.

(Chapter 7, "When One Man Rules the World," pages 142-143)

What is the significance of the 144,000 Israelites mentioned in Revelation?

During the Tribulation, God will have sent His Two Witnesses into the world to prophesy and perform mighty miracles. There will be 144,000 Israelites "sealed" for God's service during this period (Revelation 7:4). The 144,000 Israelites will become evangelists and shall see a great harvest of souls during these terrible Tribulation days. It is hard to imagine the impact 144,000 Spirit-filled Jews might have on the world. Their power from the Holy Spirit enables them to have great courage and bravery as they give witness to the Word and testify to salvation in Jesus Christ. Twelve Spirit-filled Jews turned their world upside down. Imagine the magnitude of the revival that will take place during the Tribulation.

They are 144,000 of all the tribes of the children of Israel. In the seventh chapter of Revelation, the Holy Spirit names the names of the tribes in order to avoid confusion. There are 12,000 from each tribe. They will be preserved so that they cannot be killed. People will hear their message and will be saved. The reward given to the 144,000 is for the faithfulness they exemplified in walking after God and doing what God told them to do.

It is hard to imagine the impact 144,000 Spirit-filled Jews might have on the world.

What does the Bible mean by 144,000 virgins?

In Revelation 14, the 144,000 Israelites are called virgins. The word "virgin" is not used as a physical description. As we see in 2 Corinthians 11:2, a virgin can symbolize one who has a sincere and pure devotion to Christ. These 144,000 are separated from pollution and corruption on the earth. They are virgins unto God. They have given themselves in pure devotion to the Lord. They are truly a separated and sanctified group of people. They are pure in their ministry. They are not soiled with the pollution of the world. That's the kind of witness God craves, no matter what generation we live in. The more godly we are, the more God can use us. Perhaps the greatest preparation we can make for ministry is the preparation of our own hearts in righteousness and holiness before God.

What does it mean when the Bible says the 144,000 Israelites are sealed with the mark of God?

Revelation 7:3-4 explains that the 144,000 evangelists are preserved in their ministry by the Spirit of God. They have the Father's name written prominently on their foreheads.

It is death not to have the mark of the Beast written on one's head during the time of the Tribulation. But during the Tribulation, 144,000 people will be walking around *without* 666 written on them, and they will not be dead. They will not be neutral; they will be aggressive. They won't just be walking around without the mark, they'll be walking around with their own forbidden mark. They don't want anyone to be in doubt as to who they belong to. They have God's mark on them, and it's evident to everyone.

It is death to have the mark of God, but these preachers confess Christ and are unashamed of Him. And they are preserved. They have come all the way through the Tribulation preaching the Gospel. They are all still alive. God sealed them. When you are God's person, in God's will, you are immortal until God is finished with you. God is in control. That doesn't mean that you should live life recklessly, but it means that God has committed Himself to preserve you throughout your ministry.

During the Tribulation, 144,000 people will be walking around without 666 written on them, and they will not be dead.

Will there be consequences on earth for those who worship the Beast?

Revelation 16:2 is the record of terrible sores upon those who have taken the mark of the Beast and worshiped his image. The sores reflected on these rebels symbolize that they worship Satan.

Those who have taken the mark of the Beast up until this time appear to be religious people. They identify with the great religious regime of their day. But in this awful moment of judgment when the bowls are turned over on earth, the sores will be another mark of identification to demonstrate that they are rebelling against God. It's as if God causes the poison of the rebellion within these people to surface and be manifested in sores all over their bodies.

There are also six other disasters on earth at this time. These disasters are carrying out the judgment of God. The remaining part of the sea will turn to blood, rivers and streams become blood, the sun scorches people with fire, the earth will be in darkness, the Euphrates River will completely dry up, and thunder, lightning, and hailstones weighing ten pounds will fall from the sky.

> *Then I heard a loud voice from the temple saying to the seven angels, "Go and pour out the bowls of the wrath of God on the earth." So the first went and poured out his bowl upon the earth, and a foul and loathsome sore came upon the men who had the mark of the beast and those who worshiped his image.*
> *~ Revelation 16:1-2*

Will those who worship the Antichrist experience anything like the Old Testament plagues in Egypt?

When God visited Egypt with the plagues, the sixth plague was very similar to that which takes place in Revelation 16:2. The Bible describes the plague as "boils that break out in sores on man and beast throughout all the land of Egypt" (Exodus 9:9).

It's possible that the plague of sores is a fulfillment of an Old Testament prophecy. The prophecy was given by Moses when he repeated the law before the people of Israel (Deuteronomy 28). The curse of sores was pronounced upon those who would refuse to follow the law and would follow instead after strange gods. As far as we know, this prophecy was never totally fulfilled in Israel's history. But these in the Tribulation who have followed after the Antichrist will see this prophecy fulfilled through their affliction.

The judgment that is mentioned in Revelation 16:10-11 is a plague of darkness. Once again, it is reminiscent of the plagues of Egypt. Just as the sores of the first plague are a symbol of the inner infection of those who bear them, this outer darkness is a reflection of the darkness of heart and soul of those who deny God.

Then the fifth angel poured out his bowl on the throne of the beast, and his kingdom became full of darkness; and they gnawed their tongues because of the pain. They blasphemed the God of heaven because of their pains and their sores, and did not repent of their deeds.
~ Revelation 16:10-11

What is the purpose of Armageddon?

Why would God allow such a terrible campaign to take place? First, this is the time of indignation upon the people of Israel for rejecting their Messiah and failing to heed the judgment of God. The Jews are being punished for their rebellion. Second, the nations will be judged for their persecution of the Jews. God says in Joel 3:2 that He is going to bring together all the nations that have persecuted Israel and punish them for the way they have treated His people, Israel. Third, God is going to use this as a time to judge all the nations for their sinfulness.

God is going to use this as a time to judge all the nations for their sinfulness.

What will Armageddon be like?

Israel will be the center of conflict. The battle will fill the entire land of Israel with conflict and bloodshed. Six major powers are going to be involved in the final campaign: the revived Roman Empire, the northern confederation (Russia and her allies), the kings of the East (Asia), the kings of the South (Africa), the Lord and His armies, and the nation of Israel.

A covenant will be made between the Antichrist and Israel that will bring peace and the renewal of the Jewish sacrifices to Israel for three and one-half years. The Antichrist will magnify himself (Daniel 11:36-37). Then Russia will invade Israel (Ezekiel 38). There will be a struggle between the northern and southern kingdoms (Daniel 11:40). All the nations will converge on the great battlefield of Armageddon.

At that moment the Lord will show up to set things right (Revelation 19:11). The Scriptures tell us that when the nations that are gathered together against Jerusalem see the Lord's armies coming, they will forget about each other and band together to fight against the Lord. In one dramatic moment Christ brings conclusion to the Battle of Armageddon. He throws the Beast and the False Prophet into the lake of fire and establishes His kingdom on earth.

It will take seven months to bury the dead and seven years to rid the earth of all the weapons which have been gathered by the nations (Ezekiel 39:8-16). The last verse of Revelation 14 describes a scene that is difficult to imagine: "And the winepress was trampled outside the city, and blood came out of the winepress, up to the horses' bridles, for one thousand six hundred furlongs." The blood shed at this final battle is spread over a 200-mile area (approximately the size of

Israel) and reaches a depth of four feet (the height of a horse's bridle).

In one dramatic moment Christ brings conclusion to the Battle of Armageddon. He throws the Beast and the False Prophet into the lake of fire and establishes His kingdom on earth.

Who will experience Armageddon?

Those who are left on the earth after the removal of the last Christians are those who have spurned the blood of Jesus. They have spurned the witness of the prophets who came before Jesus and the apostles who came after Him. They have spurned the Gospel message that has been spread. They have spurned the witness of the 144,000 who preached to them. They have spurned the Two Witnesses who preached to them. They have spurned the witness of the angel who flew across the skies to witness to them. There is no longer any alternative. The judgment of God is finally coming.

ACT 3

The Second Coming

To Judge the World

Following the rule of the Antichrist, it is
reassuring to know that Christ will return
to rule and reign over the earth and to judge
the world.

When Jesus arrives on earth the second time, His landing will dramatically herald the purpose of His coming. The moment His feet touch the Mount of Olives, the mountain will split apart, creating a broad passageway from Jerusalem to Jericho. As you can imagine, this will be an unprecedented geological cataclysm. Thus, Christ's return will be amplified by a devastating spectacle that will make Hollywood disaster movies look like Saturday morning child's fare. The world will see and recognize its rightful Lord and King. Whereas He came the first time in humility and simplicity, this time His glory and majesty will be spectacularly displayed for all to see.

(Chapter 10, "The Return of the King," page 220)

How will the earth be judged at the end of the Tribulation?

At the close of the Tribulation, Jesus Christ will come again to judge the earth. He will reconcile His chosen people to Himself, and the reign of the King of kings will begin. Everlasting righteousness will be brought in during the Millennium. The Temple will be anointed and the beauty of Jewish worship reestablished in the millennial Temple.

Who is the Judge?

Matthew 25:31 tells us clearly that the Son of Man is the Judge presiding over the judgment of nations. John 5:22 tells us that the Father will not judge anyone; He has committed all judgment to His Son, Jesus Christ. Not only that, but the Bible says that He will come with His holy angels to pour out His judgment.

When is the judgment?

The time of this judgment is well established by premillennial students of the Scriptures. It takes place when the Son comes in all His glory, so this judgment will be at the Second Coming. This is not the Rapture when Christians will meet Christ in the air but the Second Advent, when He will come to earth and end the Great Tribulation. This judgment will be put into effect at the end of the Tribulation and will be for all non-Jews alive at that particular time.

Where is the judgment?

This judgment will take place on earth, not in heaven. Jesus will have returned to sit on His glorious throne, and "of the increase of *His* government and peace *there will be* no end, upon the throne of David and over His kingdom, to order it and establish it with judgment and justice from that time forward, even forever. The zeal of the LORD of hosts will perform this" (Isaiah 9:7). Jesus Christ will reign over the restored earth for a thousand years (the Millennium) in His kingdom, then over a newly created heaven and earth for all eternity.

Who will be judged?

The judgment will be over all the people alive on the planet when He returns. Though He will have taken the believers into heaven at the Rapture seven years earlier, others will have come to believe in Him during that dreadful time called the Tribulation. At this time, the unsaved will go into everlasting punishment and the saved into eternal life with God. The purpose of this judgment is to see who goes into the kingdom and who goes into the lake of fire. All those who have believed in Christ during the Tribulation will reign with Him for a thousand years, and all those who have refused to believe will go immediately to hell.

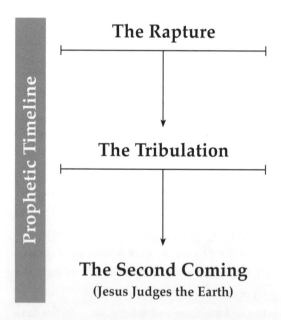

Prophetic Timeline

The Rapture

The Tribulation

The Second Coming
(Jesus Judges the Earth)

What will the Second Coming be like?

Matthew writes: "For as the lightning comes from the east and flashes to the west, so also will the coming of the Son of Man be. For wherever the carcass is, there the eagles will be gathered together. Immediately after the tribulation of those days the sun will be darkened, and the moon will not give its light; the stars will fall from heaven, and the powers of the heavens will be shaken. Then the sign of the Son of Man will appear in heaven, and then all the tribes of the earth will mourn, and they will see the Son of Man coming on the clouds of heaven with power and great glory. And He will send His angels with a great sound of a trumpet, and they will gather together His elect from the four winds, from one end of heaven to the other" (Matthew 24:27-31).

The Second Coming will be a glorious event beheld by believers and unbelievers alike. It is a cataclysmic event that will usher in the Millennium, Christ's thousand-year reign on earth.

> *The Second Coming will usher in the Millennium, Christ's thousand-year reign on earth.*

When Christ returns at the Second Coming, will we know Him?

Because the Rapture takes place before the Second Coming, we Christians will be in heaven with Christ during the Tribulation. At the time of the Second Coming we will know Him because we will be with Him when He returns.

But you are a chosen generation, a royal priesthood, a holy nation, His own special people, that you may proclaim the praises of Him who called you out of darkness into His marvelous light.

~ 1 Peter 2:9

Who will come with Christ at the Second Coming?

When Jesus returns to this earth to once and for all put down ungodly rebellion, He will be accompanied by the armies (plural) of heaven. Jude 14-15 and 2 Thessalonians 1:7-10 suggest that the armies of heaven will be populated by Old Testament saints, Tribulation saints, and the Church. They are all dressed for combat, but their attire is unusual. All of them are dressed in white, not military fatigues! They don't have to worry about their uniforms getting soiled—they never lift a finger in the battle. Jesus Himself slays the rebels with the sword out of His mouth.

Revelation mentions the Supper of God and the Marriage Supper. Which will I attend?

There are two suppers mentioned in Revelation 19. The first is the Marriage Supper of the Lamb; the second is the Supper of God, in which the flesh of the foes of God is devoured by the scavenging birds. We are given our choice as to which supper we will attend. If we do not wish to eat the food at the Marriage Supper of the Lamb, we can become the food at the Supper of God. Christians will all be at the Marriage Supper of the Lamb— they will be the Bride of Christ!

> *We are given our choice as to which supper we will attend.*

Who will be the first to experience hell?

The first two inhabitants of hell are the Beast and the False Prophet—and they are still suffering the torments of that dreadful place 1,000 years later, when Satan himself joins them in the lake of fire. All of them "will be tormented day and night forever and ever" (Revelation 20:10). Their sins are so evident and heinous that they are cast directly into hell without ever appearing at the Great White Throne Judgment described in Revelation 20.

> *The devil, who deceived them, was cast into the lake of fire and brimstone where the beast and the false prophet are. And they will be tormented day and night forever and ever.*
> *~ Revelation 20:10*

Will Christians be at the Judgment Seat or the Great White Throne Judgment?

Christians come before the Judgment Seat of Christ, not before the Great White Throne Judgment. There are about 1,007 years between the two judgments. The believers' judgment is at the beginning of the Tribulation. Then there are the seven years and the Millennium, and then comes the Great White Throne Judgment.

No one can run away from the judgment of God. Revelation 20:13 states, "The sea gave up the dead who were in it, and Death and Hades delivered up the dead who were in them. And they were judged, each one according to his works." These dead, those who have rejected Christ, come before the Great White Throne Judgment. If their name is not found in the Book of Life, they are thrown into the lake of fire (Revelation 20:11-15).

The Believers' Judgment
(The Judgment Seat of Christ)
is at the beginning of the
Tribulation

Then there are seven years
(Tribulation)

Followed by 1,000 years
(Millennium)

And then comes the
Great White Throne Judgment

> **When are the hopeless souls of the unredeemed thrown into the lake of fire?**

At the Great White Throne Judgment, every unredeemed person who has ever lived will stand before Jesus Christ to receive the sentence of eternal death. There they will all face a Judge but no jury, a Prosecutor but no defender, a sentence but no appeal. It is the final judgment of the world. There is no hope for those who appear before the Great White Throne Judgment. There is no possibility of redemption, no possibility of a favorable verdict, and no possibility of appeal. There is only one sentence, and that is to be thrown into the lake of fire.

Is my name in the Book of Life?

Everyone who is born has his name in the Book of Life. The names of those who, by faith, receive the free gift of eternal life remain in the book.

Those who do not receive God's free gift are blotted out. "Let them be blotted out of the book of the living, and not be written with the righteous" (Psalm 69:28). "And anyone not found written in the Book of Life was cast into the lake of fire" (Revelation 20:15) where the souls of the damned will languish for all eternity. There, separated from the glory of God, they will remain in an unending state of hopeless agony.

This Book of Life is mentioned frequently in Scripture (see Exodus 32:32-33; Psalm 69:28; Daniel 12:1; Philippians 4:3; Revelation 3:5; 13:8; 17:8; 21:27; 22:19) and it is imperative to make sure that your name is contained in it because that is your reservation for your eternal home with God!

He who overcomes shall be clothed in white garments, and I will not blot out his name from the Book of Life; but I will confess his name before My Father and before His angels.

~ Revelation 3:5

The Millennium

To Rule the World

The word *millennium* is made up of two Latin words. *Milli* means "one thousand" and *annum* is the word for "years." Therefore, *millennium* translates to "one thousand years." During that time, Christ will rule on earth in peace and justice from the capital in Jerusalem. The Millennium will be a foretaste of the heavenly state that is to follow.

EXCERPT FROM
THE HANDWRITING ON THE WALL:

Christ will come back when He is ready, and He will set up His kingdom without our help. That's why we need to be praying this great prayer with Isaiah: "O, that you would rend the heavens and come down" (Isaiah 64:1, NIV). On the Isle of Patmos we can say with John, "Amen. Even so, come, Lord Jesus" (Revelation 22:20). That's the only hope for lasting peace.

(Chapter 5, "When Christ Rules the World," pages 68-69)

What is the meaning of the word "millennium"?

Millennium means "one thousand years," and it derives from Revelation 20:1-6 which describes the rule and reign of Christ on earth. For a thousand years, Christ will rule as king over all the earth from His capital, Jerusalem. The saints of God, who returned with Him for the Battle of Armageddon, rule with Christ during the Millennium. We help to oversee a thousand years of peace and righteousness on earth. Satan will be bound during that period so that peace may flourish and the knowledge of the Lord may fill the earth. Everyone entering the Millennium will be a believer.

Will Christ reign on earth for a literal 1,000 years?

The duration of the Millennium is mentioned six times in Scripture and is never described in such a way as to suggest it should be taken symbolically or allegorically. The text is simple and straightforward: This earthly kingdom will last for 1,000 years (Revelation 20:1-6).

> *... Then I saw the souls of those who had been beheaded for their witness to Jesus and for the word of God, who had not worshiped the beast or his image, and had not received his mark on their foreheads or on their hands.*
> *And they lived and reigned with Christ for a thousand years.*
> *~ Revelation 20:4*

What will the Millennium be like?

There will be no war. Kingdoms will be unified. Even the animal kingdom will be at peace (Micah 4:2-3; Isaiah 11:6-9). It will be a time of unrestrained prosperity. All want will be eliminated (Isaiah 35). Sin will be kept in check, and disobedience will be swiftly dealt with in this time of great purity. Christ's kingdom will be a holy kingdom (Isaiah 11:9; 25:9; 66:23; Zechariah 13:2). During this time Satan will be bound and sealed so that he cannot go out to deceive the nations.

A man who dies at the age of 100 will be thought accursed! There will be perpetual health. It appears that the extraordinary lifespan that characterized the race before the Flood will reappear (Isaiah 65:20). The Millennium will be an exhilarating era of happiness, contentment, and personal joy.

It will be the answer to many ancient and anguished prayers (Isaiah 9:3-4; 12:3; 14:7-8; 25:8-9; 30:29; 42:1, 10-12).

EXCERPT FROM
WHAT YOU ALWAYS WANTED TO KNOW ABOUT HEAVEN:

Because of the rule of a righteous King whose justice will keep life in balance around the world, many of the causes of heartache will be removed. The Millennium will be a time of unprecedented joy as a natural by-product of peace. Isaiah 14:7 says, "The whole earth is at rest and quiet; they break forth into singing."

(Lesson 9, "What on Earth Is the Millennium," page 100)

What happens at the end of the Millennium?

During the Millennium, children will be born who will populate the earth during the Millennium. Some of these children rebel against the righteous rule of God. Satan is loosed for a time at the end of the Millennium, and he stirs up a final rebellion on earth among those who haven't believed during the thousand years. The final judgment of the world, the Great White Throne Judgment, concludes the Millennium and ushers in eternity.

At the completion of the Millennium, Christ's kingdom will continue without end as heaven comes to earth.

What is the difference between Postmillennialism, Amillennialism, and Premillennialism?

These are three competing views concerning the Millennium.

Postmillennialism teaches that the Church itself will bring about the Millennium through the preaching of the Gospel. As more and more people across the globe are converted, the world will gradually be conquered for Christ, and Jesus will at last return to earth to take up the throne won for Him by His Church.

Amillennialism teaches that there is no literal 1,000-year reign of Christ. Instead, the Church inherits the millennial blessing promised to Israel, and Christ reigns through the Church right now in an allegorized millennium. This view was developed and promoted by

Augustine in the fourth century and remains a common view in many reformed circles.

Premillennialism is the oldest view of the three and holds that Christ will physically return to earth to put down His enemies and reign over the earth for a literal 1,000-year period. This view is found in the writings of the earliest Church fathers and remains the most common view among evangelicals.

The Millennium is proof positive that Christ's death is essential for mankind's salvation.

Why should one believe in a literal Millennium (Premillennialism)?

There are at least four reasons why Christ must come back to earth to reign personally over the kingdoms of the world.

A literal Millennium is needed to reward the people of God. Scores of promises are scattered throughout both testaments guaranteeing that God's people will receive bountiful rewards for faithful service.

A literal Millennium is needed to respond to the disciples' prayer recorded in Luke 11 and Matthew 6. When they prayed, "Your kingdom come," they were requesting that the long-awaited kingdom would be established.

A literal Millennium is needed to redeem creation. Genesis 3 describes the horrors of a world cursed by God because of sin, while

Romans 8 describes a coming time when that curse will be lifted. The Millennium is the only period in history where such a lifting of the curse can be found.

A literal Millennium is needed to reemphasize man's depravity and the necessity of Christ's death on the cross. The Millennium will answer once and for all the age-old question of whether man's sin stems from environment or heritage. The Millennium will feature 1,000 years of unbroken peace and prosperity, in which Christ will rule from Jerusalem with an iron rod. Yet at the end of that age of bliss, Satan will be loosed for a short time to demonstrate that the heart of man is indeed black with sin and that even in a perfect environment, unredeemed men will turn against God and rebel. The Millennium is proof positive that Christ's death is essential for mankind's salvation.

The New Heaven and the New Earth

To Create God's Eternal Kingdom

God has established an eternal home for
His children where there will be no sickness
or dying. Former sorrows will not be
remembered as His children spend eternity in
His presence, rejoicing in the New Jerusalem.

How will all the Christians fit into one city—the New Jerusalem?

The city is laid out as a cube in dimensions so enormous it defies the imagination. Each side of the city is said to measure a staggering 1,500 miles. It will be 1,500 miles wide, 1,500 miles long, and 1,500 miles high. That is more than 2 million square miles on the first "floor" alone! The size of the Celestial City is mind-boggling—it will exceed anything that we have ever imagined in size and in beauty. The God who created all things can certainly design and build a great Celestial City that will accommodate the saints of all the ages.

And he carried me away in the Spirit to a great and high mountain, and showed me the great city, the holy Jerusalem, descending out of heaven from God, having the glory of God. Her light was like a most precious stone, like a jasper stone, clear as crystal. Also she had a great and high wall with twelve gates, and twelve angels at the gates, and names written on them, which are the names of the twelve tribes of the children of Israel: three gates on the east, three gates on the north, three gates on the south, and three gates on the west.

~ Revelation 21:10-13

Can you imagine a holy city? It will be a community where no one lied, no shady business deals were ever discussed, no unclean movies or pictures were seen. The New Jerusalem will be holy because everyone in it will be holy. Whatever discouraging or dark thoughts enter our minds today will be erased.

(Chapter 19, "Paradise Regained," page 244)

What will we do in heaven?

We will never grow bored! We will sing (Revelation 15:3-5). Those who could never carry a tune on earth will be able to sing in heaven and never grow weary of exalting the name of the King of kings. We'll serve perfectly, enabled by the power that is able to conform all things to the pleasure of His sovereign will (Revelation 1:1; 7:3; 10:7; 11:18; 15:3; 19:5; 22:6). We'll share unbroken fellowship (Revelation 19:9; Hebrews 12:18, 22-24) with God, angels, members of the Church, and the spirits of just men made perfect. Never again will we have to say goodbye to a loved one or give a farewell party. Through our resurrected bodies, we will have instant access to each other at all times.

God has different things for different people to do. God made each of us unique with a special ministry and a responsibility. Each of us in our own right has a purpose and design for what God has called us to do. There are many distinct groups in heaven, all unique in their responsibility before God. For instance, the 24 elders are crowned, enthroned, and seated (Revelation 4:10; 11:16). The 144,000 from the Tribulation have no crowns or thrones and are standing up and singing a song that no one else knows. The song of the 144,000 sounds like great rushing waters and loud peals of thunder. It is joy-filled.

When we get to heaven, we are going to praise God in every conceivable way. All of heaven is filled with music. Worship music gives us a taste of heaven. There are more hymns in the book of Revelation than in any other book of the Bible, except for the book of Psalms. Music needs to be a high priority with us if we want to know how to worship the Lord.

Is there such a thing as "soul sleep"?

Revelation 6:9-11 strikes a deathblow to the idea of "soul sleep." The souls under the altar who were martyred during the Tribulation are conscious and speaking: "And they cried with a loud voice, saying, 'How long, O Lord ....'" We should not be led astray by the use of the word "sleep" in connection with the death of the body. This is not "soul sleep." We can understand more clearly when we read 1 Thessalonians 4:14-16. Here we are told about the resurrection of the believers: (1) They rise from the grave, and (2) God will bring them with Christ when He returns. There is only one way to explain how they can both rise and be brought from heaven. The soul and the body are separated in death. "Sleep" is applied only to the believer's body, which goes into the grave and awaits resurrection. "Sleep" is NEVER applied to the soul of the believer.

Can anything keep the unsaved dead from hell?

No. That is why our primary goal is to reach as many people as possible before it is too late. There is no second chance, nor is there annihilation after death. At death, the unsaved descend immediately into Hades where they are kept under punishment until their bodily resurrection—resulting in damnation (Daniel 12:2; Luke 16:22-23; 23:43; Philippians 3:10-11, 21; Revelation 20:11-15).

> *But he said to him, "If they do not hear Moses and the prophets, neither will they be persuaded though one rise from the dead."*
>
> *~ Luke 16:31*

As a Christian, why should I not fear death?

The Bible has a unique view of death for those who have placed their trust in Jesus Christ. It describes death for the believer as *precious*. "Precious in the sight of the LORD *is* the death of His saints" (Psalm 116:15). The Bible also describes death for the believer as being without sting. "O Death, where *is* your sting? O Hades, where *is* your victory?" (1 Corinthians 15:55) It also describes death as "be[ing] with Christ." "For I am hard-pressed between the two, having a desire to depart and be with Christ, *which is* far better" (Philippians 1:23). In heaven you will see Jesus face-to-face— "And God shall wipe away every tear from their eyes; there shall be no more death, nor sorrow, nor crying. There shall be no more pain, for the former things have passed away" (Revelation 21:4). This is the wonderful hope with which we live!

How can I apply the truths of prophecy to my life?

Such a careful writer as John is not likely to leave us wondering how we ought to apply the message of Revelation. He makes his purposes for writing the book crystal clear. You can be blessed just by reading the book (Revelation 1:3; 22:7) or cursed for tampering with it, according to Revelation 22:18-19. The road to true success, Revelation tells us, is found in submitting our lives to God's Word. Revelation teaches us that although someday the need for evangelism will disappear, the need and privilege of worship is eternal. Practice down here before we worship Him perfectly up there!

We are under the same instruction that John received to take the words of the Gospel to men and women, boys and girls who do not yet know and love the Savior. And Paul said,

"For we must all appear before the judgment seat of Christ, that each one may receive the things *done* in the body, according to what he has done, whether good or bad" (2 Corinthians 5:10).

We must make ourselves ready and watch for His coming because we have received ample warning that He is coming and there will be no time to prepare: "… Surely I am coming quickly …" (Revelation 22:20).

For additional information from Dr. Jeremiah on this subject, please order "What To Do Until Then" from volume 4 of the *Escape the Coming Night* series.

EXCERPT FROM
ESCAPE THE COMING NIGHT:

Now we reach the end of our journey and will be given a preview of eternity future; a new heaven and a new earth will be created. Although it is difficult to imagine anything more wonderful than the heaven we inhabit upon our deaths, the eternal heaven will be even more glorious. The crowning jewel in paradise will be the holy city, the New Jerusalem.

(Chapter 19, "Paradise Regained," page 241)

CONCLUSION

The study of prophecy is very important—we need to know what God has planned for us. However, some people desire to learn everything about the End Times, but they don't go far enough into the study of our Lord's Word to realize that He also gave us some responsibilities to fulfill.

We are to do business until He comes. We are not to be apathetic, passive, sit-around-on-our-hands people. In light of the fact that the Lord could come at any moment, we are to be busy about the Lord's work.

Some of our Lord's final words before going back to heaven concerned the importance of evangelizing those who do not know Him. In Acts 1:6-8, His instructions are so clear that we cannot mistake what He said:

> Therefore, when they had come together, they asked Him, saying, "Lord, will You at this time restore the kingdom to

Israel?" And He said to them, "It is not for you to know times or seasons which the Father has put in His own authority. But you shall receive power when the Holy Spirit has come upon you; and you shall be witnesses to Me in Jerusalem, and in all Judea and Samaria, and to the end of the earth."

These words are a simple echo of the Great Commission given by our Lord in Matthew 28:18-20, when Jesus said to His disciples, "All authority has been given to Me in heaven and on earth. Go therefore and make disciples of all the nations, baptizing them in the name of the Father and of the Son and of the Holy Spirit, teaching them to observe all things that I have commanded you; and lo, I am with you always, *even* to the end of the age."

Jesus gave us our orders, and these words should be the first concern of every Christian. Not only are these the last words of our Lord but they are also His first words upon entering into His public ministry. In Matthew 4:19: "Then He said to them, 'Follow Me, and I will make you fishers of men.'"

In between these two statements, of course, were many other words from the lips of our Lord. For instance, Luke 19:10: "For the Son of Man has come to seek and to save that which was lost."

In Mark 10:45, when James and John came to the Lord to request a place of prominence in the kingdom, Jesus used His own life as an example by saying, "For even the Son of Man did not come to be served, but to serve, and to give His life a ransom for many."

When Jesus was giving His great message on the bread of life, He declared, "For I have come down from heaven, not to do My own will, but the will of Him who sent Me. This is the will of the Father who sent Me, that of all He has given Me I should lose nothing, but should raise it up at the last day" (John 6:38-40).

In Jesus' famous meeting with Nicodemus, when the ruler came to Him one night, He said, "As Moses lifted up the serpent in the wilderness, even so must the Son of Man be lifted up, that whoever believes in Him should not perish but have eternal life" (John 3:14-15).

And in John 10:10 our Lord said, "I have come that they may have life, and that they may have *it* more abundantly."

Anyone who listens to the words of the Lord Jesus catches the passion of His heart. His last words to us were, "… you shall be witnesses to Me in Jerusalem, and in all Judea and Samaria, and to the end of the earth" (Acts 1:8) and "… Go into all the world and preach the gospel …" (Mark 16:15) and "… lo, I am with you always …" (Matthew 28:20). His first words upon entering into His public ministry on this earth were "Follow Me, and I will make you fishers of men" (Matthew 4:19). That is the passion of His heart.

If the Lord Jesus were here today to speak to His people, what would He say? I think He would say what He said the first time He walked on this earth in public ministry. I think He would say the last words He said before He went back to heaven. I think He would say to all of us, "Men and women, learn all you can about the future; but don't forget, you are My witnesses, and you are to go into all the world and preach the Gospel to every creature." If evangelism is buried by eschatology, it is an unworthy grave.

When it was time for Jesus to select the men who would follow Him and carry on His ministry, He didn't give them a temperament test. The Scriptures say that when Jesus selected those who would follow Him, He carefully chose men who would do what He did. He didn't say, "Come after Me, and I will make you founders of the Church." He didn't say, "Come after Me, and I will make you experts in prophecy." From the very first day they began to follow Jesus Christ, each disciple knew in his heart exactly what his purpose was. He was called to be a fisher of men. He was called to be an evangelist, to tell others about Jesus Christ.

Sometimes we need to go back and read the directions again—to go back to the simplicity of what Jesus told us to do. Maybe we have become a little too sophisticated. Maybe we have forgotten that the primary plan in Jesus' heart when He instructed His disciples is still the primary plan in His heart for the Church of Jesus Christ today.

The disciples got the message early. They waited obediently in Jerusalem until the Holy Spirit came upon them, and then they went out to follow the orders of their ascended Commander-in-Chief. In just a few short years, they fulfilled the promise of Christ that they would do greater things than He had done. Starting with a handful of men on the Day of Pentecost, that group of disciples grew and multiplied until, at the end of seven years, conservative estimates say their number totaled more than 100,000 souls! No wonder the apostles were accused of turning the world upside down.

People say they filled Jerusalem with His doctrine. So well did they adhere to the divine purpose that within 300 years, the whole Roman Empire was undercut and overthrown by the power of the Gospel of Jesus Christ. Everywhere they went, they shared the life of Jesus that had so transformed their hearts.

Notice what happened to those early churches. The Early Church was one throbbing heartbeat of purpose. In Paul's letter to the Romans, he said, "... I thank my God through Jesus Christ for you all, that your faith is spoken of throughout the whole world" (Romans 1:8).

When he wrote to the church in Thessalonica, it was somewhat similar. He said, "... you became examples to all in Macedonia and Achaia who believe. For from you the word of the Lord has sounded forth, not only in Macedonia and Achaia, but also in every place. Your faith toward God has gone out, so that we do not need to say anything" (1 Thessalonians 1:7-8). Paul was saying in effect, "We came here to evangelize; but because of you, it's already here. We don't have to say a word. Everywhere you've gone, Jesus Christ has been the theme, He's been the subject, He's been the source, He's been the one everyone's talked about."

If we know everything there is to know about prophecy but we haven't the time to walk across the street and introduce our neighbor to the Lord or to bring someone to church to hear the Gospel, we are not following our Lord's last instructions. The last command of our Lord was His first concern: to go into all the world and preach the Gospel to every creature.

While we are about our Lord's business sharing the Good News, we are to live in hope and expectation of His return. He is the source of hope in this dark world. And if you don't yet know Him, you too can know Him in a personal way. Follow the Romans Road to Salvation, and pray to ask Christ to become your Lord and Savior.

"Amen! Come, Lord Jesus!" (Revelation 22:20, HCSB).

Walk Down the

ROMANS ROAD TO SALVATION

God loves you!

For God so loved the world that He gave His only begotten Son, that whoever believes in Him should not perish but have everlasting life.
John 3:16

God has a wonderful plan for your life!

I have come that they may have life, and that they may have it more abundantly.
John 10:10b

1. Because of our sin, we are separated from God.

For all have sinned and fall short of the glory of God.
Romans 3:23

2. The penalty for our sin is death.

For the wages of sin is death, but the gift of God is eternal life in Christ Jesus our Lord.
Romans 6:23

3. The penalty for our sin was paid by Jesus Christ!

But God demonstrates His own love toward us, in that while we were still sinners, Christ died for us.
Romans 5:8

4. If we repent of our sin, then confess and trust Jesus Christ as our Lord and Savior, we will be saved from our sins!

For "whoever calls on the name of the LORD shall be saved."
Romans 10:13

If you confess with your mouth the Lord Jesus and believe in your heart that God has raised Him from the dead, you will be saved. For with the heart one believes unto righteousness, and with the mouth confession is made unto salvation.
Romans 10:9-10

5. Can you be sure that if you ask Christ to save you, He will?

Whoever believes that Jesus is the Christ is born of God ... These things I have written to you who believe in the name of the Son of God, that you may know that you have eternal life ....
1 John 5:1, 13

But as many as received Him, to them He gave the right to become children of God, to those who believe in His name.
John 1:12

TOPICAL INDEX

Numbers

A

B

bowls, 76, 77

H

I

J

judgment, 13, 14, 15, 16, 17, 21, 29, 30, 34, 35, 39, 42, 49, 53, 54, 64, 76, 77, 79, 80, 84, 89, 90, 91, 98, 99, 100, 101, 111, 127

L

lake of fire, 26, 82, 83, 91, 98, 99, 101, 102

M

Matthew, 14, 19, 23, 24, 25, 26, 30, 37, 67, 89, 93, 114, 131, 132, 133, 134

Millennium, 14, 17, 66, 89, 91, 94, 99, 100, 105, 107, 108, 109, 110, 111, 112, 113, 114, 115

Moses, 46, 47, 50, 78, 124, 133

N

New Jerusalem, 117, 118, 120, 128

T

W

ADDITIONAL
RESOURCES

Escape the Coming Night

Come along with Dr. Jeremiah on an electrifying tour of the world as it races toward its final days. This chapter-by-chapter study of the book of Revelation takes you through End Times prophecy, from the events on earth to the drama in heaven and back to the spectacular creation of a new earth.

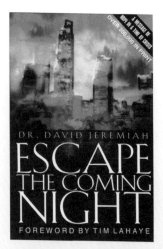

The Handwriting on the Wall
Secrets From the Prophecies of Daniel

More than "the man in the lion's den" or "the dreamer," Daniel shows us how to live today and how to face the future with confidence and joy. Join Dr. Jeremiah as he takes an in-depth look at the book of Daniel.

Revelation Prophecy Chart
A Panorama of Prophecy

This Turning Point timeline reference to the book of Revelation is a colorful, easy-to-use, fully illustrated chart designed to identify the course of prophetic events as chronicled in the book of Revelation.

Agents of the Apocalypse

In *Agents of the Apocalypse*, you will become acquainted with the ten most prominent players in the book of Revelation—those who are the primary agents of the apocalypse. Each chapter opens with an engaging, biblically based dramatization that brings prophecies to life as never before. This book reveals the overarching truth of Revelation—that the Christian's victory in Christ is an absolute certainty.

Agents of Babylon

In *Agents of Babylon*, noted prophecy expert, David Jeremiah, explores the many prophecies, dreams, and visions outlined in the book of Daniel through the lens of its central characters, then carefully explains what they mean, and shows us how they apply to the world today so that we can better prepare for the future.

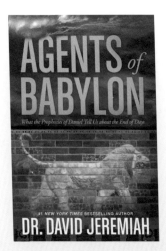

Revealing the Mysteries of Heaven

Revealing the Mysteries of Heaven closes the gap between what the Bible says about heaven and what the average believer knows. By studying the Scriptures from Genesis to Revelation and studying a variety of topics, the curtain is pulled back—to the extent Scripture allows—to reveal the glorious and utterly amazing realm of heaven.

People Are Asking …
Is This the End?

The world seems more fractured each day. People are asking, "Is this the end?"

No one can afford to ignore these warnings, but all can better understand the greater story and the role we each play in this changing world. From prophetic clues in Scripture to an understanding of the power of Christ in all believers, this book directs us on a clear path forward.

About David Jeremiah

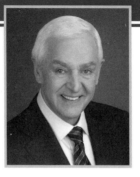

Dr. David Jeremiah serves as senior pastor of Shadow Mountain Community Church in El Cajon, California. He is the founder and host of *Turning Point*, a ministry committed to providing Christians with sound Bible teaching relevant to today's changing times through radio and television, the Internet, live events, resource materials, and books. A best-selling author, Dr. Jeremiah has written more than fifty books including *Captured by Grace*, *Living with Confidence in a Chaotic World*, *What*

in the World Is Going On?, *The Coming Economic Armageddon*, *Agents of the Apocalypse*, and *People Are Asking … Is This the End?*

Dr. Jeremiah's commitment to teaching the complete Word of God continues to make him a sought-after speaker and writer. His passion for reaching the lost and encouraging believers in their faith is demonstrated through his faithful communication of biblical truths.

A dedicated family man, Dr. Jeremiah and his wife, Donna, have four grown children and twelve grandchildren.

THE MALE ANIMAL

CLEMSON MEMORIAL
LIBRARY
MONARCH IN A

The Male Animal

/3

A Play by

JAMES THURBER

and

ELLIOTT NUGENT

GUERNSEY MEMORIAL
LIBRARY
NORWICH N.Y.

With Drawings by

JAMES THURBER

RANDOM HOUSE · NEW YORK

FIRST PRINTING

*All rights reserved. No part of this book
may be reproduced in any form without the permission of Random House, Inc.*

CAUTION: Professionals and amateurs are hereby warned that *The
Male Animal,* being fully protected under the copyright laws of
the United States of America, the British Empire, including the
Dominion of Canada, and all other countries of the copyright
union, is subject to royalty. All rights, including professional,
amateur, motion picture, recitation, lecturing, public reading,
radio broadcasting, and the rights of translation into foreign lan-
guages, are strictly reserved. Particular emphasis is laid on the
question of readings, permission for which must be secured from
the authors in writing. All inquiries should be addressed to the
authors, in care of Herman Shumlin, Selwyn Theatre, New York
City.

Inquiries regarding the semi-professional and amateur acting rights
and the stock rights of this play should be addressed to Samuel
French, 25 East 45th Street, New York City, or 811 West 7th
Street, Los Angeles, California, and in Canada to Samuel French
(Canada) Limited, 480 University Avenue, Toronto.

Photographs by Vandamm Studio

CUYAHOGA MEMORIAL
LIBRARY
NORWICH R A

COPYRIGHT, 1940, BY JAMES THURBER AND ELLIOTT NUGENT

PUBLISHED SIMULTANEOUSLY IN CANADA BY THE MACMILLAN CO.

PRINTED IN THE UNITED STATES OF AMERICA

47604

The Male Animal was produced by Herman Shumlin at the Cort Theatre, New York City, on January 9, 1940, with the following cast:

In order of appearance

Cleota	AMANDA RANDOLPH
Ellen Turner	RUTH MATTESON
Tommy Turner	ELLIOTT NUGENT
Patricia Stanley	GENE TIERNEY
Wally Myers	DON DE FORE
Dean Frederick Damon	IVAN SIMPSON
Michael Barnes	ROBERT SCOTT
Joe Ferguson	LEON AMES
Mrs. Blanche Damon	MINNA PHILLIPS
Ed Keller	MATT BRIGGS
Myrtle Keller	REGINA WALLACE
Nutsy Miller	RICHARD BECKHARD
Newspaper Reporter	JOHN BORUFF

Staged by HERMAN SHUMLIN

Setting designed by ALINE BERNSTEIN

Costumes supervised by EMELINE CLARK ROCHE

Time: The present.

The scene of the play is the living room of the Turners'
house, in a Mid-Western college town.

ACT ONE: A Friday in late fall, evening.

ACT TWO:
Scene I. The next day, after lunch.
Scene II. Three hours later.

ACT THREE: Two days later.

ACT ONE

ACT ONE

SCENE: *The living room of a pleasant, inexpensive little house. There is no distinction of architectural design, but someone with natural good taste has managed to make it look attractive and liveable on a very modest budget. There are some good prints on the walls. The hangings are cheerful, and the furniture, picked up through various bargains and inheritances, goes together to make a pleasing, informal atmosphere.*

The front door opens onto a porch. The wall is lined with bookshelves which continue around the corner to the fireplace. Below this fireplace is a stand with a radio-phonograph. In the center of the rear wall is a bay window with window seat. This corner is used by the Turner family as a casual depository for visitors' hats and coats, although they have also a coat-rail just inside the front door. In front of the bay window, a long table backs a comfortable couch. To the right of the bay window are more bookshelves, a small landing, and a stairway running up and off-stage. In the corner below the stair near the dining-room door a table has been prepared today to serve as a temporary bar, with a tray, cocktail shaker, and two or three bottles and glasses. On the right there are two doors, one leading to the dining room, the other to another porch and the back yard. Two small sofas, an armchair, a couple of small end or coffee tables, and one or two straight

3

chairs complete the furnishings of the room. There are two or three vases of flowers, and the books and magazines which frequently litter this room have been put tidily away.

At the rise of the curtain, the phone on the table behind the sofa is ringing. CLEOTA, *a colored maid, enters from the dining room and answers it.*

CLEOTA

Professah Turner's res-i-dence. . . . Who? . . . You got de wrong numbah. . . . Who? . . . What you say? . . . Oh, Mistah *Turner!* No, he ain' heah. He jus' went out to buy some likkah. . . . Who is dis callin'? Yessuh. Yessuh. Ah doan get dat, but Ah'll tell him Doctah Damon. Ah say Ah'll tell him. (*She hangs up phone, starts for dining room.*)

ELLEN'S VOICE
(Upstairs)

Who was it, Cleota?

CLEOTA

It was Doctah Damon. He say he comin' ovah to see Mistah Turner or Mistah Turner come over to see him, or sumpin'. (*She turns on lights from wall switch.*)

ELLEN
(Coming downstairs)

What was that again, Cleota? (*She is an extremely pretty young woman about twenty-nine or thirty. Quick of speech and movement, she has a ready smile and a sweetness of personality that warms the room. She is completely feminine and acts always from an emotional, not an intellectual stimulus.*)

4

THE MALE ANIMAL

CLEOTA

Doctah Damon doan talk up. He kinda muffles.

(ELLEN *begins to put finishing touches to the room with quick efficiency, putting away magazines and books.*)

ELLEN

I'm afraid it's you that kind of muffles.

CLEOTA

Yessum. Miz Turner, Ah'm fixin' dem whore doves for the pahty. Did you say put dem black seed ones in de oven?

ELLEN

Black seed ones? Oh, heavens, Cleota, you're not heating the caviar?

CLEOTA

No'm, Ah ain' heatin' it, but taste lak' sumpin' oughtta be done to it.

ELLEN

It's to be served cold. Here, you pick up the rest of the magazines. I'll take a look at the canapés. (*Hurries off into dining room.*)

CLEOTA

Yessum. Ah ain' no hand at 'em. People where Ah worked last jus' drank without eatin' anything. (*There is the sound of whistling outside, and* TOMMY TURNER *enters. He is a young associate professor, thirty-three years old. He wears glasses, is rather more charming than handsome. His clothes are a little baggy. He has a way of disarranging his hair with his hands, so that he looks like a puzzled spaniel at times.*

5

He is carrying chrysanthemums and two bottles of liquor, wrapped in paper and tied with string) Oh, hello, Mr. Turner.

TOMMY

Hello, Cleota.

CLEOTA

You bettah not mess ּיֹם dis room 'cause dey is guess comin'.

TOMMY

All right, Cleota. I'll be good.
 (CLEOTA *gives him a doubting look and dawdles off to dining room. We see what she means when* TOMMY *unwraps his packages. In a moment, paper and string drop about him like falling leaves. Manfully, he sticks flowers in the vase among the other flowers. A book with a gay jacket catches his eye. He looks at it disapprovingly, throws it in wastebasket.* ELLEN *enters from dining room.*)

ELLEN

Hello, dear.

TOMMY

Hello, Ellen. Those are for you. (*Indicates his flowers.*)

ELLEN

Oh, thank you, Tommy. They're lovely. (*Surveys the flowers.*)

TOMMY

The ones in the middle.

6

ELLEN

Yes . . .

TOMMY

I got the liquor, too.

ELLEN

(*Taking flowers out of vase*)

Did you get the right kind?

TOMMY

I got both kinds.

(ELLEN *picks up the litter he has made.*)

ELLEN

Tommy, you're a house-wrecker, but you're nice. (*Kisses him.*)

TOMMY

Did I do something right?

ELLEN

Cleota! Cleota, will you fill this vase with water, please? (*Hands vase to* CLEOTA *in doorway.* CLEOTA *goes out*) What became of the book that was on this table?

TOMMY

That? Oh, I threw it in the wastebasket. It's trash.

ELLEN

(*Rescuing book*)

But you can't throw it away. Wally gave it to Patricia.

TOMMY

Oh, he did?

ELLEN

Besides, it's just the right color for this room.
(*Young voices are raised outside and* PATRICIA STANLEY, ELLEN'S *sister, opens the door and backs into the room. She is a pretty, lively girl of nineteen or twenty. She is followed by* WALLY MYERS, *who is six-feet-one, and weighs 190 pounds, mostly muscle.*

PAT'S VOICE

Oh, Wally, quit arguing! I'm going to dinner with Mike,

8

and then to the rally with you. You can't feed me at the training table.

WALLY

Aw, that guy Barnes! I don't see why you have to . . . Oh, how do you do, Mrs. Turner—Professor Turner?

TOMMY

Hello, Butch.

ELLEN

That's Wally Myers.

WALLY
(*To* PATRICIA)
Oh, has Butch been coming here, too?

PATRICIA

Go on, get out of here, half-back. I have to get dressed. (*As she sits down and inspects a run in her stocking*) Hey, Ellen, excited about seeing the great Ferguson again? He just drove up to the Beta House in a Duesenberg!

(CLEOTA *re-enters with the vase; gives it to* ELLEN *and leaves.*)

ELLEN
(*Arranging* TOMMY's *flowers*)
Did you see him?

PATRICIA

No, the kids were telling me. Has he still got his hair?

ELLEN

I haven't seen him in ten years. We'll soon find out.

9

WALLY

Say, is he coming here?

ELLEN

Yes. Why don't you come back and meet him, Wally? You can tell him all about the game tomorrow.

WALLY

Gee, thanks! But nobody could tell Joe Ferguson anything about a football game. He's all-time All-American, you know. Well, thanks, Mrs. Turner. I'll be back. See you later, Pat. (WALLY *goes out.*)

TOMMY

Does he mean that now Joe belongs to the ages, like Lincoln?

ELLEN

Um-hum, in a way.

TOMMY

(*Crossing to bookcase*)

Well, I suppose he has passed into legend. I used to admire him myself—almost.

ELLEN

Pat, why don't you and Michael stay here for dinner? Supper, rather. It's just a bite. We're all going out to eat after the rally.

PATRICIA

No, thanks. You know Michael hates Mr. Keller. He'd spit in his eye.

TOMMY

Why do we have to have Ed Keller to this party? (*Carrying three copies of* Harper's, *he sits on settee.*)

10

ELLEN

Oh, Joe has to have someone to talk football with. Besides, Ed's his closest friend here. He practically paid Joe's way through college. You can stand the Kellers one night.

TOMMY

Just barely. I don't know how to entertain trustees.

PATRICIA

You'd better be entertaining tonight with the great Ferguson coming. (*Rises*) Weren't you engaged to him once, Ellen?

ELLEN

Not officially. Just for fun.

PATRICIA

(*Going upstairs*)

Baby, that can be dangerous, too!

ELLEN

Oh, Dean Damon phoned, Tommy.

TOMMY

What'd he want?

ELLEN

I don't know. Cleota answered the phone.

TOMMY

Oh . . . I see. . . . Oh, I'll bet I know what it was. I saw him this morning. What do you think?

ELLEN

Oh, I don't know . . . Oh, Tommy, you don't mean . . . ?

TOMMY

Yes, I do.

ELLEN

Oh, Tommy, that's wonderful! It's three hundred and fifty more a year, isn't it?

TOMMY

Five hundred! I'm no piker.

ELLEN

Well, you certainly deserve it. (*Gives him a little kiss.*)

TOMMY

Now I can get you that fur coat next February. People must think I let you freeze in the winter.

ELLEN

(*Crossing to table*)

No, they don't. And, don't worry about me—you need some new things yourself. . . . I love the flowers, Tommy. And this promotion couldn't have come on a better day for me. Do you know what day it is?

TOMMY

Friday, isn't it? Why?

ELLEN

Oh, nothing—never mind. (*Glances around room*) What became of all the match boxes? I had one in each ash tray. (*She returns and digs in his coat pocket.*)

12

TOMMY

I haven't seen any match boxes. What's going on here? Say, you look very pretty tonight. That's a new dress, isn't it?

ELLEN

No. It's my hair that's bothering you. It's done a new way.

TOMMY

Doesn't bother me. I like it.

ELLEN

(*Who has found two match boxes*)

One more.

TOMMY

Oh, you exaggerate this match-box thing. Oh. (*Hands her one*) I ought to take you out to dinner more and show you off.

ELLEN

(*Redistributing match boxes*)

Well, we're going out tonight after the rally.

TOMMY

I mean just the two of us. Tonight will be just like old times. Remember how Joe was always horning in on our dinner dates? I don't believe we ever had one that he didn't come over and diagram the Washington Monument play or something on the tablecloth with a pencil.

ELLEN

Statue of Liberty play, darling.

TOMMY

He was always coming. I never saw him going.

ELLEN

There's still one missing.

TOMMY

I haven't got it. (*He finds it*) I'll bet Joe does something to get his wife down. Probably cleans his guns with doilies. Clumsy guy. Always knocking knives and forks on the floor.

ELLEN

He wasn't clumsy. He was very graceful. He was a swell dancer. (*She puts away some books.*)

TOMMY

I remember he got the first and the last dance with you the last time we all went to a dance together.

ELLEN

Phi Psi Christmas dance, wasn't it?

TOMMY

No, the May dance. Out at the Trowbridge Farm. Remember how it rained?

ELLEN

I remember I had the last dance with Joe because you disappeared somewhere.

TOMMY

No, I was watching—from behind some ferns.

14

ELLEN

They played "Three O'Clock in the Morning" and "Who?"
It was a lovely night, wasn't it?

TOMMY

No, it poured down. You and Joe were dancing out on the
terrace when it started. You both got soaked, but you kept
right on dancing. (*Having found what he wanted*, TOMMY
returns two magazines to shelves.)

ELLEN

Oh, yes, I remember. My dress was ruined.

TOMMY

You were shining wet—like Venus and Triton.

ELLEN

Why didn't you cut in? (*Takes magazine* TOMMY *left on
coffee table to bookcase.*)

TOMMY

I had a cold. Besides, my feet hurt. (*He starts toward stairs*)
I'll dress. (*Doorbell rings*) Lord, I hope he isn't here already.
  (ELLEN *admits* DAMON *and* MICHAEL. DAMON, *the head of
  the English department, is a tall, thin, distinguished-
  looking man of some sixty-five years. He has gray
  hair, eyes capable of twinkling through glasses whose
  rims he has a habit of peering over. He talks slowly,
  selecting his words, in a voice at once compelling and
  humorous. He often hesitates, peers over his glasses
  before saying the last word of a phrase or a sentence.*

15

THE MALE ANIMAL

MICHAEL BARNES *is a senior in the Arts College, an intensely serious young man and a fine literary student. The older people who surround him find his youthful grimness about life's problems sometimes amusing, but more frequently alarming.*)

ELLEN

Oh, come in, Dr. Damon. Hello, Michael.

MICHAEL

How do you do?

TOMMY

How do you do, sir?

DAMON

Hello, Thomas.

ELLEN

Where's Mrs. Damon?

DAMON

I shall pick her up and bring her along shortly for the festivities. This is in the nature of an unofficial call.

TOMMY

Hello, Michael. You both look a little grim. Has anything happened?

DAMON

Michael has written another of his fiery editorials.
(PATRICIA *runs down the stairs.*)

PATRICIA

Ellen, did you see my— Oh! How do you do, Dr. Damon? Hi, Michael.

16

MICHAEL

H'lo.

DAMON

Sit down, my dear. I have here an editorial written by Michael for *The Lit,* which comes out tomorrow. Perhaps, to save time, one of us should read it aloud. . . .

"When this so-called University forces such men out of its faculty as Professor Kennedy, Professor Sykes, and Professor Chapman, because they have been ignorantly called Reds, it surrenders its right to be called a seat of learning. It admits that it is nothing more nor less than a training school"—(you will recognize the voice of our good friend, Hutchins, of Chicago)—"a training school for bond salesmen, farmers, real-estate dealers, and ambulance chasers. It announces to the world that its faculty is subservient. . . ." (DAMON *peers over glasses at* MICHAEL.)

MICHAEL

Oh, I didn't mean you, of course, Dr. Damon.

DAMON

". . . that its faculty is subservient to its trustees, and that its trustees represent a political viewpoint which must finally emerge under its proper name, which is—Fascism."

PATRICIA

Oh, Michael! There you go again!

DAMON

Wait till you hear where he has actually gone.

17

PATRICIA

Isn't that all?

DAMON

Unhappily, there is more.

PATRICIA

Oh, Lord!

(TOMMY *sits down.*)

DAMON

(*Continuing*)

"These professors were not Reds. They were distinguished liberals. Let us thank God that we still have one man left who is going ahead teaching what he believes should be taught."

TOMMY

Who's that?

DAMON

Sh! "He is not afraid to bring up even the Sacco-Vanzetti case. He has read to his classes on the same day Vanzetti's last statement and Lincoln's letter to Mrs. Bixby." (I hope we are not alienating the many friends of Abraham Lincoln.) (TOMMY *rises and glances at* MICHAEL *questioningly*) "The hounds of bigotry and reaction will, of course, be set upon the trail of this courageous teacher, but, if they think they are merely on the spoor of a lamb they are destined to the same disappointment as the hunters who, in chasing the wild boar, came accidentally upon a tigress and her cubs. Our hats are off to Professor Thomas Turner of the English Department." That's all.

ELLEN

Tommy?

TOMMY

Michael, I think you might have consulted me about this.

PATRICIA

Michael, you fool! They'll kick you out of school for this—and Tommy, too!

ELLEN

You never told me you had brought up the Sacco-Vanzetti case in your classes, Tommy.

DAMON

Yes, just what is this Vanzetti letter you have read?

TOMMY

I haven't read it yet.

MICHAEL

When you told me the other day you were going to read it, I thought you meant that day.

TOMMY

No, Michael, I just meant some day. But I was talking to you as a friend, I was not giving an interview to an editor.

ELLEN

But why were you going to read this letter, Tommy?

TOMMY

Because it's a fine piece of English composition, and I'm

19

teaching a class in English composition. An obscure little class. I don't want any publicity, Michael. I just want to be let alone.

ELLEN

But, Tommy, nobody thinks of Vanzetti as a writer.

TOMMY

It happens that he developed into an extraordinary writer. I don't think you could help being interested in the letter yourself, Dr. Damon.

DAMON

You would be surprised at my strength of will in these matters, Thomas. What I am interested in is preserving some air of academic calm here at Midwestern—and also in retaining my chair in the English department.

PATRICIA

You don't want to get Tommy kicked out of school, do you, Michael?

MICHAEL

No. I didn't think of that. I thought Mr. Turner was about the only man we had left who would read whatever he wanted to to his classes. I thought he was the one man who would stand up to these stadium builders.

TOMMY

I'm not standing up to anyone, Michael. I'm not challenging anyone. This is just an innocent little piece I wanted to read.

(MICHAEL *turns away*.)

20

ELLEN

(*Rises*)

I know it must be all right, Tommy, but you can't read it now. Keller and the other trustees kicked Don Chapman out last month for doing things just as harmless as this. (*Turning to* MICHAEL) You'll have to change that editorial, Michael.

MICHAEL

I can't. The magazines were run off the presses last night. They've already been delivered to the newsstands.

DAMON

They go on sale in the morning. (*To* ELLEN) I think that our—er—tigress here may have to issue a denial tomorrow. After all, he hasn't read it.

ELLEN

(*To* TOMMY)

Yes, and you mustn't read it now.

PATRICIA

Will Michael be kicked out of school, Dr. Damon?

DAMON

Sufficient unto the day is the evil thereof, my dear. (*He gets his hat.*)

PATRICIA

(*To* MICHAEL)

There! You see—

21

DAMON

(Coming to TOMMY *who has seated himself at the other side of the room)*

I quite understand how you meant to present it, Thomas, but our good friend, Mr. Keller, would not. Do not underestimate Mr. Edward K. Keller. He rolls like the juggernaut over the careers of young professors.

TOMMY

I know.

DAMON

(Starting to door)

Well—since he must be with us tonight let us confine our conversation to the woeful inadequacies of the Illinois team.

TOMMY

(Rising)

Oh, it isn't Illinois we're playing—it's Michigan.

DAMON

Oh, I must remember that. *(Goes out.)*

PATRICIA

(To MICHAEL*)*

There, you see! You will be kicked out.

MICHAEL

He didn't say that.

PATRICIA

Yes, he did. Don't come back for me, Michael. I'm staying here for supper. *(Runs up the stairs.)*

GUERNSEY MEMORIAL
LIBRARY
NORWICH N Y

GUERNSEY MEMORIAL
LIBRARY
NORWICH N Y

MICHAEL

I see. . . . I'm sorry, Mr. Turner. I guess I got—well—carried away.

TOMMY

(*Crossing*)

I know, Michael. Sometimes, when I see that light in your eye I wish I could be carried away too.

MICHAEL

Yes, sir. (*He goes out grimly. There is a slight pause.*)

TOMMY

Well—

ELLEN

I'm sorry, Tommy.

TOMMY

Oh, it's all right. Maybe I can read this thing later on, after all the fuss quiets down—say, next spring.

ELLEN

It would still be dangerous.

TOMMY

Yes, I guess it would. . . . I know I'm not a tiger, but I don't like to be thought of as a pussycat either.

ELLEN

(*With an understanding smile*)

It's getting late. You'd better go and put on that gray suit I laid out for you.

23

TOMMY

Yeh, sure. (*Crosses to stairs.*)

ELLEN

And be sure your socks are right side out, and, Tommy—don't try to be a tiger in front of Ed Keller.

TOMMY

(*At stair landing*)

I won't. I'm scared of those Neanderthal men. I'll talk about football.

ELLEN

Thank you, darling. That's swell. You know how Joe is—always cheerful. And we do want it to be a good party.

TOMMY

(*Starting upstairs*)

I'll be cheerful. I'll be merry and bright. I'll be the most cheerful son-of-a-gun in this part of the country. (*He disappears. We hear him singing a snatch of "Who's Afraid of the Big Bad Wolf?" The doorbell rings.*)

ELLEN

Hurry, Tommy! They're here! (*Crosses to the door and admits* JOE FERGUSON, *followed by* WALLY MYERS) Hello, Joe!

JOE

Ellen! How are you, baby? God, you look great! Why, you're younger and prettier than ever! If I were a braver man, I'd kiss you. Doggone it, I will kiss you! (*Kisses her*

24

on cheek, hugs her, lifts her off the floor—whirls her around.
WALLY *closes door.* JOE *is all that we have been led to expect:
big, dynamic, well dressed, prosperous. He is full of good nature and a boundless enthusiasm for everything.*)

ELLEN
(*Catching something of his ebullience*)
It's terribly nice to see you again, Joe. If I were a younger
woman, I'd say it's been all of ten years.

JOE
(*Whipping off his coat, he puts down a small box on sofa*)
Gosh, this is swell! Where's the great Thomas?

ELLEN
Tommy will be right down. I see Wally found you—so
you've met?

JOE
Yeh. We joined forces outside.
(WALLY *hangs up* JOE's *coat.*)

ELLEN
(*At settee*)
Come on over here and sit down.

JOE
I forgot to ask you, Wally, who's going in at the other half
tomorrow? Stalenkiwiecz?

WALLY
No, sir. Wierasocka.

25

JOE

Really?

WALLY

He's a Beta. From Oregon.

JOE

Oh, yeh—yeh, I know.

WALLY

Stalenkiwiecz is laid up. They think he's got whooping cough. (*He sits in center of settee beside* ELLEN.)

JOE

That's bad! I've got a thousand fish on that game. (*Sits on settee. It is very crowded.*)

WALLY

I think it's safe, all right, Mr. Ferguson, but I wish we had you. Stalenkiwiecz, Wierasocka, Myers and Whirling Joe Ferguson.

ELLEN

Do they still call you Whirling Joe?

JOE

Oh, sure, remember how—

WALLY

Say, he was the greatest open-field runner there ever was.

ELLEN

Yes. Joe, why haven't you ever been—

26

WALLY

Why, you made Red Grange look like a cripple.

JOE

Well, they say you're not so bad yourself. Say, Ellen, how's—

WALLY

Aw, I'm just fair, that's all. (*Produces a clipping*) This is what Grantland Rice said about me. (*Hands it to* JOE.)

JOE
(*Beginning to wish* WALLY *would go*)
Yeh. Too bad this is Wally's last year. We're going to miss him—eh, Ellen?

ELLEN
(*Pointedly*)
Have you got anything to do, Wally?

WALLY

Coach wants me to help him with the backfield next season. Not much money in it, of course.

JOE
(*Hands clipping back to* WALLY)
Well, if you want my advice, don't go in for coaching. I had a sweet offer from Cincinnati in twenty-nine. Remember that, Ellen?

ELLEN

I remember very well. Do you remember when—

27

WALLY

Nineteen twenty-nine! I was only twelve years old then.

TOMMY

(*Coming downstairs*)

Hello, Joe! It's nice to see you again!

JOE

(*Rises and shakes hands*)

Tommy, old man, how are you? Ten years! Teaching must be good for you. And Ellen, here, looks like a million bucks! That reminds me—I came laden with gifts. (*Turns and almost runs into* WALLY. *He recovers and gets the small box*) These are a few flowering weeds. . . .

ELLEN

(*Opening the box of orchids*)

Oh, thank you, Joe. They're lovely. Tommy, will you call Cleota?

TOMMY

Sure. (*Goes to dining-room door, calls*) Cleota!

ELLEN

It's fun to get flowers. Very festive.

JOE

Oh, it's nothing much, but I wanted you to know I remembered the great day. Think I'd forget it was your birthday?

28

ELLEN

You never used to. (TOMMY *has rejoined them*) Tommy gave me some flowering weeds, too—for my birthday.

TOMMY

Yes, I got her some—for your—oh—yes. . . . Not such nice ones, I'm afraid. (*To* ELLEN) I'm a lucky man.
(CLEOTA *enters.*)

ELLEN

Will you find something to put these in, Cleota?

CLEOTA

Ah'll hafta put 'em in de sink wit dat ice. (*Goes out with flowers.*)

JOE

Boy, it's sure great to be here!

TOMMY

It's nice to have you. . . . Staying long?

JOE

Got to be in Washington next week. Well, Tommy, I see you've still got a lot of books.

TOMMY

Oh, yes.

JOE

You know I never get a chance to read books. (*He sits on settee again.*)

WALLY

Say, you must have a swell job! (*He sits on bench before fireplace.*)

JOE

By the time I get through at night, I'm lucky if I can keep up with what's going on in the world. Way things are changing, you gotta do that. I take fifteen magazines. That keeps me busy.

ELLEN

(*Linking an arm through* TOMMY's)

Tommy's had several articles in *Harper's* and the *Atlantic*.

JOE

No! Say, that's fine! But you'll have to boil them down to *The Reader's Digest* to reach me, Tommy. You know, that's a great little magazine.

TOMMY

Do you like bullion cubes?

ELLEN

(*Hastily*)

Tommy, you'd better make a drink.

TOMMY

Yes. We have a lot of celebrating to do. (*He goes out to dining room, calling* CLEOTA.)

ELLEN

How've you been, Joe? (*Sits next to* JOE.)

JOE

Fine, except for a little sinus trouble.

WALLY

You know, Mrs. Turner, I recognized him right away from that big picture in the gym.

(TOMMY *re-enters with bowl of ice, mixes drinks at table.*)

ELLEN

That's fine. How's Brenda? I meant to ask before.

JOE

Fine! Great! Little heavier, maybe. We're being divorced, you know.

ELLEN

But I didn't know. Oh, Joe, I'm sorry.

JOE

Nothing to be sorry about. It's just one of those things.

TOMMY

What's the matter?

ELLEN

Joe and his wife are breaking up.

TOMMY

Oh, that's too bad.

JOE

No, it's all fine. We're both taking it in our stride. Took her out to dinner last week—along with her new boy friend.

31

TOMMY

Wasn't that rather complicated?

ELLEN

Oh, you're not up to date, Tommy. That's the modern way of doing things.

JOE

Sure. Take it in your stride. Gosh, Ellen, I can't take my eyes off you. (*At* WALLY's *chuckle,* JOE *rises and changes the subject*) Nice little place you got here. Need any help, Tommy? I'm a demon on Manhattans. (*He is starting toward* TOMMY *when the doorbell rings.*)

TOMMY

I'm all right, thanks.

JOE

I hope that's Ed, the old scoundrel.
(ELLEN *admits the* DAMONS.)

ELLEN

I'm so glad— Hello, Mrs. Damon.

BLANCHE

Hello, Ellen, dear. How do you do, Mr. Turner?

ELLEN

You must know Joe Ferguson.

BLANCHE

Oh, of course. How do you do?
(JOE *bows, smiling.*)

32

ELLEN

This is Mrs. Damon, Joe. And you remember Dean Damon?

JOE

Yes, indeed. Nice to see you again, sir.

DAMON
(*Crossing to him and shaking hands*)
Back for the slaughter of the—uh—Michigan innocents, eh?

JOE

That's right.
(ELLEN *and* BLANCHE *have turned to* WALLY.)

ELLEN

Mrs. Damon, may I present Mr. Myers?
(BLANCHE *shakes hands with him.*)

WALLY

How do you do?

BLANCHE

Oh, yes, of course we all know about our great full-back.
(TOMMY *gives* JOE *a cocktail.*)

ELLEN

Let me help you with your coat.

BLANCHE

Thank you, dear. (*To* WALLY) Tell me, are you nervous about the game tomorrow?

33

WALLY

No, ma'am.

BLANCHE

Not the least little bit?

WALLY

No, ma'am.

BLANCHE

That's nice. (*Smiling at his surprise, she sits on settee.*)

DAMON

(*To* JOE)

I remember you not only from the gridiron but from my Shakespeare class. You slept very quietly.

JOE

I never did finish reading *Hamlet*. I always wondered how that came out. (*He laughs heartily;* DAMON *laughs politely.*)

TOMMY

Does anybody mind a Manhattan?

BLANCHE

Oh, Ellen. Could we have sherry?

ELLEN

Certainly. Tommy . . .

(TOMMY, *who is bringing two cocktails to the* DAMONS, *pauses uncertainly.*)

34

TOMMY

Sherry coming right up. Here, Wally. (*Gives him cocktail.*)

WALLY

No, thanks. I'm in training.

TOMMY

Well, just hold it. Sherry for you, too, Dr. Damon?

DAMON
(*Disappointed*)

When Mrs. Damon says we, she means me. Sherry, thanks.
(TOMMY *drinks the left-over cocktail.*)

BLANCHE

A little sherry is such fun. (WALLY *offers her a cigarette from the box on the coffee table*) No, thanks, I'll smoke my Spuds.
(WALLY *lights* BLANCHE'S *cigarette.*)

PATRICIA
(*Coming downstairs*)

Hello, everybody.

ELLEN
(*Presenting* PAT *to* JOE)

This is my sister, Patricia.

PATRICIA

How do you do?

JOE

(*Admiring her*)

How do you *do?* My goodness! Why, you're as big and pretty as your sister. How about a drink?

PATRICIA

No, thanks. (*To* ELLEN, *as she crosses to* WALLY) Still has his hair. Hello, Wally.

(TOMMY *serves sherry to the* DAMONS.)

WALLY

Hi, Pat. Look, can I pick you up at Hennick's a little earlier?

PATRICIA

I'm not going to Hennick's. I'm eating here. That date's off.

WALLY

With Barnes? Say, that's swell. . . . I got to run along, Mrs. Turner. Nice party. (*Crosses to* JOE) Glad I met you, Joe—I mean, Mr. Ferguson. (*They shake hands*) I'll be seeing you. Good-bye, everybody. I'll go out the back way. (*He goes out the door which leads into the garden.*)

JOE

Take it easy, old man. Don't break a leg on me. Remember, I've got a thousand fish on that game. (*Follows* WALLY *out.*)

WALLY

I won't.

36

BLANCHE

He's a handsome boy, Patricia. (*Doorbell rings*) And seems very healthy.

PATRICIA

I have to keep in training for him. (PATRICIA *and* DAMON *sit down on the bench before the fireplace.*)

TOMMY
(*Going to door*)

I'll get it.

(ELLEN *joins* TOMMY *and greets the* KELLERS *as they come in.* ED KELLER *is a big, loud, slightly bald man of about thirty-eight, heavy around the middle. He is a prosperous real-estate man, owns the Keller Building, is a trustee and as such is the biggest voice and strongest hand on the board.* MYRTLE KELLER, *also in her late thirties, dresses well and is not bad looking, was once pretty, but is now a slightly faded blonde.*)

ED

Hello, Ellen! Hi, Turner! Where is he? (*He passes* TOMMY *fast, without a handshake, looking for* JOE *who reappears. The two men run to meet each other. This is a typical meeting between two old friends of the hale-and-hearty, back-slapping persuasion who haven't met for years*) Hiya, you old rascal! Hahya, boy?

JOE
(*As they clinch in the middle of the room, hugging, slapping backs, etc.*)

37

Hello, you old son-of-a-gun! How are you, Ed? (*He goes to* MYRTLE) Hello, Myrtle. Gosh, I'm glad to see you! (*He hugs her, lifting her off her feet.*)

MYRTLE
(*Screams*)
Oh! I'm glad to see you, too! Ellen . . .

JOE
(*Returning to* ED)
Gee, you're looking swell, Ed, old boy, old boy!

38

ED

Judas Priest, this is swell! How are you anyway, Joe?
(*The men's voices predominate.*)

JOE

Fine! Swell! Never better. You've put on a little weight, eh, Eddie? And what's happened to the crowning glory?

ED

Worry: real-estate, Roosevelt. Wonder I got any left.

MYRTLE

How do you do, Dr. Damon? How do you do, Mrs. Damon? Haven't seen you in a long, long time. Hello, Patricia. . . . (*She sits beside* MRS. DAMON) Oh, quiet down! Ed! Are we late, Ellen?

ELLEN

Not at all. Just in time for the canapés.

JOE

How long's it been, Ed? Seven, eight years, isn't it?

ED

Eight, anyway.

ELLEN

Look, you two, break it up and say hello to people!

ED

All right, Ellen, but it sure is fine to see the Whirler again.

How do you do, Dr. Damon? Not drinking straight Scotch, I hope?

DAMON

If I did that, my stomach—and Mrs. Damon—would punish me severely.

ELLEN

Won't you have a cocktail, Ed? (*Brings drink to* ED.)

ED

Thanks.

JOE

Say, this is Ellen's birthday. How about a little toast?

TOMMY

Well, fill 'em up. (*He pours drinks, including one for himself.*)

ED

Well, happy birthday, Ellen. (*He starts "Happy Birthday to You," and they all sing. It is obvious* TOMMY *is bored; he sits down, sips his drink, then noticing everybody standing, he rises and sings the last line very off key.* CLEOTA *enters, comes up behind* DAMON *with a plate of canapés.*)

CLEOTA
(*After their song dies*)

Whore doves?

40

DAMON
(*Startled*)
I beg your pardon—oh! Thank you.

JOE
(*As* TOMMY *pours another round*)
Let's drink one toast to The Big Red Team. What do you say? (TOMMY *starts humming "The Big Bad Wolf."*)

ED
The Big Red Team!

TOMMY
(*Singing softly to himself*)
"The Big Red Team—
Big Red Team.
Who's afraid of The Big Red Team . . ."

ED
What's that?

TOMMY
Huh? (ED *glares at him. To* ELLEN) What did I do?

ELLEN
Tommy, you'd better eat something. Those cocktails are strong.

TOMMY
I'm doing all right, honey. How's everything in Detroit, Joe?

41

JOE

I don't know. All right, I guess. (ED *and* JOE *seat themselves on settee away from the women.*)

ELLEN

Tommy means Pittsburgh. The Bryson Steel Company is in Pittsburgh, Tommy. (CLEOTA *gives* ELLEN *the tray and goes out.*)

TOMMY

Oh, yes, sure. Well, how's everything in Pittsburgh?

JOE

Well, it might be worse.

ED

Couldn't be much worse out here.

TOMMY

Have a drink.

ELLEN

(*Takes canapés to* MYRTLE)

How are the kids, Myrtle?

MYRTLE

They're all right. The baby has some kind of rash on her little hips, but it's nothing, really. Makes her cross, though.

ED

Time sure does fly. Now Buster wants to go to Princeton.

42

No matter how you watch 'em, they get in with the wrong kids.

(*The women's voices predominate.*)

BLANCHE

How's your sister?

MYRTLE

They took a stone out of her as big as a walnut. She can't weigh more than ninety pounds.

JOE

I remember when I actually got along with only one car, and thought it was plenty. Now I've got three, and the bills are terrific. . . . Do you know what my gas bill was last month? . . .

(DAMON *rises, bored, picks out a book and glances through it.*)

BLANCHE

They cut old Mrs. Wilmot open for the same trouble, and didn't find a thing!

MYRTLE

Ed, when was it I had that impacted tooth out?

ED

Seven years ago. Year the banks closed. Thirty-three.

TOMMY

Fill 'em up. (*Pours himself another.*)

ELLEN

Tommy! (*She takes shaker away from him*) Dividend for the women folks. Give me your glass, Myrtle.

43

MYRTLE

Thanks.

BLANCHE

No more for us. Mercy, we'd be light-headed.

TOMMY

(*Following* ELLEN, *takes shaker from her, pours himself another*)

But we're celebrating: the homecoming game, banks closing and everything.

JOE

How's building out here now, Ed?

TOMMY

(*Sauntering over to the men*)

Yeh, how's building?

ED

Lousy. Whatta ya expect with that man in the White House? You know what *I* think? I think he's crazy.

JOE

You know what I heard?

(*The women stop their talk to listen, but* JOE *whispers in* ED'S *ear.*)

ED

I wouldn't be a damn bit surprised!

(TOMMY *puts down shaker.*)

(ED'S *voice predominates in the following:*)

44

ED

Only hope for business I see is this war. And he'll probably do something to ruin that.

BLANCHE

(*Sotto voce*)

Patricia, may I see the little girl's room?

MYRTLE

Me, too.

PATRICIA

Yes. I'll show you.
(*They start toward stairs.*)

MYRTLE

(*As they start upstairs*)

Is it serious?

BLANCHE

They took a pint of pus out of her!
(*Men react to this. The women go off, still chattering.*)

MYRTLE

Why, what's the matter with her?

BLANCHE

They don't know. They just hold consultations.
(TOMMY *and* ELLEN *sit on the long sofa to listen. She quietly takes the drink from his hand.*)

ED

Well, Dr. Damon, we men on the Board of Trustees are certainly glad that this Red scare is over.

45

DAMON

No doubt you are.

ED

Now maybe the new stadium project will get somewhere.

DAMON
(*Eagerly moving toward* ED)
And the Endowment Fund?

ED

Yeh, sure—that's important too. I'm working to convince the substantial alumni that we've got all this Parlor-Pink business over and done with. Got 'em all weeded out.

JOE

Yeah—all that newspaper stuff was pretty bad.

ED

Sure. Nobody felt like coming through for anything when they read about men like Kennedy and Sykes and Chapman being on the faculty. That Chapman was nothing but a damn Red.
(DAMON *covers his disgust and turns to* ELLEN.)

TOMMY

No, he wasn't, Mr. Keller. Don Chapman was a humanist.

ELLEN
(*Laying a quieting hand on* TOMMY's *arm*)
We knew him very well.

46

JOE

How do you know he wasn't a Red, Tommy?

ED

He went to Soviet Russia for his vacation once, didn't he?

TOMMY
(*Rising*)

He just went to see the Drama Festival.

ED
(*Suspiciously*)

Well, it's a mighty long way to go to see a show.

CLEOTA
(*Who has just entered*)

Suppah is se'ved. (*Retires to dining room.*)

ELLEN
(*Rising*)

Shall we go into the dining room? It's only a salad. We're going out to eat afterwards. Come along, Ed, we don't want to miss that rally. (*She links her arm through* ED's, *and they go out to dining room.*)

ED

Say, that's right. I haven't missed a Michigan rally in seventeen years!

(ELLEN *re-enters, goes to stairs, calls:*)

47

ELLEN

Supper's ready!

(PAT, BLANCHE, *and* MYRTLE *come downstairs.*)

BLANCHE

Thank you. Come, Frederick. (DAMON *and* BLANCHE *go into dining room.*)

ELLEN

Patricia, you get a plate for Mr. Ferguson. He's the guest of honor, you know.

JOE

And I'll get a plate for you, Ellen. Come on. (JOE *and* PAT *follow the* DAMONS.)

MYRTLE

(*As she goes into the dining room*)

Oh, what a lovely table, Ellen!

(*During the following scene until* ED's *re-entrance, there is the general conversation in the dining room, as everybody is finding his supper and beginning to eat.*)

ELLEN

(*Crossing to* TOMMY)

Tommy, don't say any more about Don Chapman tonight, please.

TOMMY

All right, I won't. Let's get something to eat. (ELLEN *takes his arm. They start for dining room*) Joe looks better, doesn't he?

ELLEN

Better?

48

TOMMY

Well, bigger anyway.

(*They exit.* CLEOTA *has entered with a clean-up tray. She clears away drinks and canapés, singing, "I Can't Give You Anything But Love" softly. She finds one glass with some liquor in it. After a long scrutiny she raises it to her lips.*)

ED

(*Off-stage*)

Come on, Myrtle. Hurry up. Joe's got to speak at this rally.

(CLEOTA *drinks and quickly puts glass on tray and resumes song as* ED *enters with plate of food. He plants himself in the center of a settee, and also takes possession of a coffee table.* BLANCHE *and* MYRTLE *enter, with* DAMON *following them and carrying two plates.*)

BLANCHE

Come, Myrtle, sit over here with me. Frederick, put it down over there on that table.

MYRTLE

(*As they cross the room*)

What makes you think there was something suspicious about it?

(*The women settle themselves on settee.*)

BLANCHE

Well, his family wouldn't allow a post-mortem. Thank you, Frederick, that's fine.

(ELLEN *and* JOE *come in.*)

ELLEN

I hope you can all find a place to sit.

JOE

(*Crossing to long sofa*)

What's the matter with this? Come on, Ellen, give me a break.

(ELLEN *smiles and sits beside him, then speaks to* PATRICIA, *who appears in dining-room door.*)

ELLEN

Pat, is Tommy getting some food?

PATRICIA

Yeh, he's all right. (*She joins the women and* DAMON, *who is eating standing up at the mantel.*)

TOMMY

(*Entering*)

Sure, I'm fine. (*He looks around for a place to settle.*)

ELLEN

Bring in the coffee, please, Cleota.

(CLEOTA *nods and goes out.*)

ED

There's room here for somebody.

TOMMY

No, thanks, I'll sit—(*Looks around for any place away*

50

from ED; *the only vacant spot is a chair beside* ED's *settee*)
—here.

MYRTLE

Eat your vegetables, Ed.

ED

Aw, this is a party.

BLANCHE

Where's Michael Barnes this evening, Patricia? Frederick tells me he's written a remarkable editorial. (DAMON *drops his fork*) Be careful, Frederick!

ED

Barnes? Barnes? I haven't read a decent editorial since Brisbane died.

PATRICIA

Michael couldn't come. He doesn't like Mr.—er—

MYRTLE

Doesn't like what?

PATRICIA

Doesn't like parties.

BLANCHE

I'm always so interested in *The Literary Magazine*. What was the editorial, Patricia?

DAMON

Eat your dinner, my dear. Remember, Mr. Keller—wants to get to the rally.

ED

Huh?

BLANCHE

(*Staring at him*)

What's the matter with you? (*He shushes her. To* PAT) I hope I haven't said anything, dear. (PAT *shakes her head.*) (CLEOTA *enters with coffee and serves the guests.*)

ED

What's going on over there? Who is this Barnes?

TOMMY

One of Patricia's beaux.

ED

Some writer?

TOMMY

He's a student. Editor of *The Literary Magazine.*

ED

Oh, yeah, I've heard of him. What's he done now?

ELLEN

Oh, it's nothing, really.

TOMMY

Well, since it's come up, Ellen, we might as well tell Mr. Keller. He'll read about it tomorrow. . . . (ELLEN *rises*) I told Michael I was going to read something to one of my English classes, and he got a mistaken idea about it and wrote a sort of—

52

ELLEN
(*Breaking in quickly*)
Just a silly little editorial—that's all.

ED
I see.

PATRICIA
Because Tommy isn't really going to read it at all.
(MYRTLE *murmurs to* BLANCHE, *rises and goes to dining room.*)

ED
What was it this kid said you were going to read? Anything important?

TOMMY
(*After a moment*)
It's a short, but beautifully written piece of English by Bartolomeo Vanzetti.

ED
Never heard of him. (*Then, as the name registers*) Hey, you don't mean Vanzetti of Sacco and Vanzetti?

TOMMY
Yes, the same man.

ED
You mean you're going to read something *he* wrote?

TOMMY
Yes, I was going to.

53

ELLEN

(*Quickly*)

But now he's not—Michael didn't understand.

ED

Why would you ever think of such a dumb thing in the
first place?

(TOMMY *has lost any appetite he may have had. He
rises and puts his plate and cup on the table.*)

TOMMY

It's part of a series. I read many such letters to my class.

ED

You mean letters by anarchists?

TOMMY

(*Restrains himself*)

No, letters by men who were not professional writers—like
Lincoln, General Sherman . . .

ED

Well, it's a damn good thing you changed your mind.
Putting Lincoln and General Sherman in a class with Vanzetti! Wouldn't look very good.

JOE

What's this?

ED

Wait a minute. (*To* TOMMY) Is this thing going to be
printed? This editorial?

54

DAMON

We discovered it too late to stop it.

ED

And this kid didn't submit it to the publications committee?

DAMON

Unfortunately, he did not. Ellen, dear, Mrs. Damon and I must be running along.

ELLEN

Oh, I'm sorry.

DAMON

I have a committee meeting.

BLANCHE
(*Astonished*)

What committee?

DAMON

Come, Blanche.

BLANCHE
(*Rising*)

Oh, yes, that little committee.

ED

Well, I hope this thing's not too bad. You better deny it quick, Turner. I tell you! I'll call the papers in the morning.

TOMMY

No, I'll take care of it.

55

JOE

(Rises)

What's going on here?

MYRTLE

(Enters from dining room with two dishes of sherbet)
Here's some sherbet, Ed.

ED

Put it down there. *(To JOE)* I'm just telling Turner here we've had enough of this Red business among the students and the faculty. Don't want any more.

TOMMY

(Returning to his chair)
This isn't Red, Mr. Keller.

ED

Maybe not, but it looks bad. We don't want anything Red —or even Pink—taught here.

TOMMY

But who's to decide what is Red and Pink?

ED

We are! Somebody's got to decide what's fit to teach. If we don't, who would?

DAMON

I thought that perhaps the faculty had . . .

ED

No, sir. You fellows are too wishy-washy. We saw that in

56

the Chapman case. Americanism is what we want taught here.

JOE

Americanism is a fine thing.

TOMMY

Fine. But how would you define Americanism?

ED

Why—er—everybody knows what Americanism is! What do you believe in?

TOMMY

I believe that a college should be concerned with ideas. Not just your ideas . . . or my ideas, but all ideas.

ED

No, sir! That's the *trouble* . . . too damn many ideas floating around. . . . You put ideas of any kind into young people's heads, and the first thing you know, they start believing them.

DAMON

On the contrary. I have been putting ideas into young people's heads for forty-two years with no—visible—results whatever.

(*There is a dubious laugh from* BLANCHE.)

BLANCHE

Come, Frederick. Good night, Ellen. Lovely party. (*She bustles* DAMON *out the door.*)

57

ED

(*Rises*)

Turner, you better think twice before you read anything. I can promise you the trustees will clamp down on any professor who tries anything funny! I'm telling you that for your own good.

JOE

Say, I thought we were going to have some fun. Let's break this up. How about some music? (*He goes over to Victrola and puts on a record.*)

ED

That's right. We're celebrating tonight. Just wanted to get that out of my system. (*He picks up the dish of ice*) Oh, I didn't want this—I wanted some of that ice cream. (*He starts for the dining room.*)

MYRTLE

He means he wants both. Here, I'll show you. (*She follows him out.*)

> (PATRICIA *starts to go, too;* ELLEN, *worried about* TOMMY, *stops her, whispering to her.* PAT *nods and turns to* JOE, *who is looking through the records.*)

PATRICIA

I'll bet you'd like some ice cream, too, Mr. Ferguson.

JOE

No, I . . . (PATRICIA *winks at him; he glances at* TOMMY) Oh, sure. Sure, I would.

PATRICIA

(*Linking an arm through his*)

Can you still skip?

58

JOE

No—not at my age. (*They go into the dining room,* PAT *closing the door softly.* TOMMY *pours himself a drink.*)

ELLEN

Tommy, have you had too much to drink?

TOMMY

No. Not enough.

ELLEN

Your eyes have that funny look.

TOMMY

Did you hear what Mr. Keller said to me? I don't like to be talked to like that.

ELLEN

Just because he was nasty and you've had a few drinks. . . . (*Goes to him*) Tommy, you're not going to go ahead and read that letter?

TOMMY

Yes, Ellen, I think I have to.

ELLEN

Tommy, try to be practical for once. At least wait until you're not so mad. Try to think of this the way any other man would think of it.

TOMMY

I'm not any other man.

ELLEN

Well, try to be. Do you think Joe would do something that

would get him into trouble just because somebody irritated him?

TOMMY

Joe! I don't see why you don't try to understand how *I* feel about this.

ELLEN

I'm simply trying to keep you out of a lot of trouble. I don't see why—

TOMMY

But you see how Joe would feel. That's very plain to you, isn't it?

ELLEN

Yes, it is. Joe wouldn't get all mixed up.

TOMMY

I'm not mixed up. I'm trying to understand what goes on in your mind. It *can't* be like Joe Ferguson's mind!

ELLEN

Oh, you and your mind! (*Turns away, exasperated*) I have to go through such a lot with your mind!

TOMMY

Maybe you wouldn't if you understood it better.

ELLEN

Oh, I know, I know! I'm too dumb for you!

TOMMY

Now, Ellen, I didn't say that.

60

ELLEN

You said Joe and I were stupid.

TOMMY

I said he was.

ELLEN

But he isn't. He's a big man. In some ways he's smarter than you.

TOMMY

Well, you ought to know. (*He turns away from her.*)

ELLEN

(*Catching his arm*)

Oh, look, Tommy—what are we fighting about?

TOMMY

(*Turns*)

You said I was dumb.

ELLEN

Tommy, you've had too many drinks or you wouldn't say that.

TOMMY

No, I haven't, but I don't feel very well. I feel very unhappy and slightly sick.

ELLEN

I'll get you some bicarbonate of soda.

TOMMY

(*Crossing to the stairs*)

No, you won't. I'll go upstairs and lie down for a few

minutes, myself. I can do that. Let's not bring this down to the level of bicarbonate of soda. (*He starts up slowly, then suddenly feels squeamish and makes a mad dash for it.* ELLEN *hesitates for a minute at the foot of the stairs—calls after him.*)

ELLEN

Tommy. Tommy, I didn't—
> (JOE *comes from the dining room with a dish of ice cream.*)

JOE

Anything the matter?

ELLEN

Oh—no. Tommy's not feeling well. He got sick once before at a party. He's not used to drinking, and he's very sensitive about it. (JOE *nods and goes to turn off the Victrola.* CLEOTA *comes in, starts clearing away supper plates.* ELLEN *goes to her, speaks in a low voice*) Cleota, will you get Mr. Turner some bicarbonate of soda from the kitchen? (CLEOTA *nods, retires to the dining room*) Cleota will get him some bicarbonate of soda from the kitchen. He'd never find it upstairs.

JOE
> (*Takes off the record and hunts for another one to his liking*)

Why wouldn't he? Where do you keep it?

ELLEN

In the medicine chest.

JOE

What was that stuff between him and Ed?

ELLEN

Oh, it's nothing, really. I'll tell you about it tomorrow. (*Her mind is on* TOMMY, *upstairs.*)

JOE

Fine. . . . Say, look what I found! "Who?" Remember that, Ellen? (*He puts the record on, starts it.* ELLEN *moves closer to the Victrola and listens as it plays:*)

"Who-o-o stole my heart away?

Who-o-o makes me dream all day?

Dreams I know can never come true.

Seems as though I'd ever be blue.

Who-o-o means my happiness . . ."

(*As naturally as if they were always dancing to this song, they both begin to dance*) Gee, this takes me back . . . the May dance. Remember?

ELLEN

Um-huh—it rained.

JOE

You said you didn't know it was raining. I know I didn't. (*Holds her closer.*)

ELLEN

(*Breaks away*)

I'm a little rusty, Joe. I haven't danced in—oh, I don't remember when. Makes me feel young.

63

JOE

Then what are we stopping for? Come on.

ELLEN

Well—all right. (*They go back into the dance. Dreaming,* ELLEN *glances up at* JOE. *They slow down to a stop and stand looking at each other, he ardently, she caught up in the music.*)

JOE

I can answer all those questions. . . . No one but you. (*As the music goes into the instrumental reprise,* JOE *kisses her, and she kisses back for a long moment, then tries to pull away.*)

ELLEN

(*As he tries to kiss her again*)

Oh, no, Joe, please, I . . . Say, how many cocktails did *I* have? (*They stand for an instant, looking at each other.*)
(*Off-stage we hear:*)

MYRTLE

Ed, come away from that ice cream. You've had enough. (JOE *and* ELLEN *quietly start dancing again, smiling.*)

ED

Oh—all right.
(TOMMY, *a little pale and disheveled, comes down the stairs and sees them dancing there; he stops;* MYRTLE *and* ED *enter.*)

MYRTLE

(*Nudging* ED)

Look, Ed! Just like the old days, isn't it? Seeing them dancing together?

ED

I'll say. (*Then, loudly*) They make a darn' handsome couple, don't they?

> (TOMMY, *although he has not seen the kiss, has sensed the whole intimacy of the scene and the meaning of* ED's *remark; he nods soberly.*)

JOE

She dances like a dream.

ED

(*Chuckling*)

Like a "dream can never come true," eh, Joe? You look mighty sweet in there, boy.

(ELLEN *sees* TOMMY. *Following her glance,* ED, MYRTLE *and* JOE *turn and look at* TOMMY.)

ELLEN

(*Breaking away*)

Oh—Tommy—are you all right?

TOMMY

(*Coming down*)

Yes, thanks. . . . Don't—let me spoil the party.

ED

Party's breaking up anyway, Tommy.

(JOE *turns off Victrola.*)

TOMMY

I just thought I'd get some more air. . . . (*Crosses to the door which leads out to the garden.*)

ED

I don't want to miss any of that rally. (*A band is heard in the distance, approaching. Holds out* MYRTLE's *coat*) Myrtle! (MYRTLE *crosses to him.*)

66

(PATRICIA *enters from dining room with bicarbonate of soda in glass.*)

PATRICIA

Who's this for, Ellen?

ELLEN

Tommy. (*To* TOMMY, *as he stands with his back turned, breathing the fresh air*) Tommy, will you take this bicarbonate?

TOMMY

Just—put it by for a moment. You go to the rally, Ellen. . . . I'm going to walk around out here—until I feel better. Good night, everybody. . . . You're coming to lunch tomorrow, aren't you, Joe?

JOE

Yes, sir!

TOMMY

That's what I thought. (*He goes out, closing the screen door.* PATRICIA *looks out the window; the band is heard louder.*)

PATRICIA

Ellen! It's the team and the band and a lot of the kids! They must be going in the Neil Avenue gate!

ED

Come on, let's step on it!

JOE

Yeh. (*Listens to music*) Boy, that sounds good! God, doesn't that take you back?

67

MYRTLE

Where'll we go after the rally?

JOE

I'll take you all to the Dixie Club! Whatta ya say, Ellen?

ELLEN

Oh, I haven't been there in years! It would be fun. . . .
But, no, I'm not going. (*Calls*) I'm going to stay here with
you, Tommy.

TOMMY
(*Off-stage*)
No, I'd rather you didn't—really.

PATRICIA
(*As music gets much louder*)
Hey! They're stopping in front of the house!
(WALLY *runs in as the music stops.*)

WALLY

Ready, Pat?

PATRICIA

Sure!
(*Breathless and excited,* WALLY *goes to* JOE.)

WALLY

Look, we brought the band over to escort you to the chapel,
Mr. Ferguson! You're going to ride in the Axline Buggy!

ED

The Axline Buggy!

WALLY

We hauled it out of the trophy room! We got two horses—not the old black ones, but we got two horses! Whatta ya say?

ED

Fine! Fine!
(NUTSY *runs in, dressed in a band-leader's uniform and carrying his glistening baton.*)

NUTSY

Hey, come on! Let's get going! The carriage waits, Mr. Ferguson! (*Does drum major's salute and clicks heels.*)

WALLY

This is Nutsy Miller, the leader of the band.

JOE
(*Shaking hands*)

Hiya, Nutsy?

NUTSY

Hiya, Joe?

JOE

Okay, fellas! Whatta ya say, Ellen—you ride with me. Some fun, huh?

ELLEN
(*In the spirit of it*)

Oh—all right. Hurray!

69

JOE

Hit her, Ed!

ED, JOE, WALLY, ELLEN, PATRICIA, NUTSY
(*Sing*)
"And if we win the game,
We'll buy a keg of booze,
And we'll drink to old Midwestern
Till we wobble in our shoes."
(*They all go out,* JOE *and* ELLEN *the center of the gay,
excited group, arm in arm. A shout goes up as* JOE
appears outside. You hear a triple "rah-team" for
JOE.)

VOICES
(*Outside*)
Rah-rah-rah!
Rah-rah-rah!
Rah-rah-rah!
Ferguson! Ferguson! *Ferguson!*
(*The band starts another march.* TOMMY *has reappeared
in the lower door a moment after the general exit.
He crosses slowly and closes upper door. The cheers
for* FERGUSON *and the band music slowly die away
as* TOMMY *turns and sees the glass of soda. He picks
it up, looks at it in distaste—distaste for himself.*)

TOMMY
Rah-rah-rah! (*He throws down the spoon, crosses to the
Victrola and starts the record.*)

70

VICTROLA

". . . Dreams I know can never come true. . . ."
(TOMMY *listens for a moment, then makes awkwardly, solemnly, a couple of dance steps, frowns, shakes his head, and drops onto settee, giving it up. He drinks the bitter cup of soda as the music ends and the*

Curtain Falls

ACT TWO

ACT TWO

Scene I

The Turners' living room—same as Act I.
About one o'clock the following day.

AT RISE: JOE, *with coat off, is arranging plates, knives,*
saucers and forks on the floor in the form of a football forma-
tion. The end table has evidently been used for serving lunch-
eon as it still holds a plate and cup. ELLEN *is seated center,*
finishing her coffee and watching JOE. PATRICIA *is down on her*
knees on the floor studying the array of dishes, napkins, salt
cellars, and glasses which are ankle-deep around JOE. CLEOTA
enters from the dining room, carrying an empty tray. She
crosses to the end table, begins clearing away the dishes, keep-
ing a suspicious eye on JOE *and the black magic he is up to.*)

JOE

Now here—it's a balanced line. Move those two men out a
little more. (PAT *moves the men out*) This is a wonderful
play! The coach gave it to me in the strictest confidence.

ELLEN

Cleota, did you phone Mr. Turner's office again?

CLEOTA

(*At end table, clearing away dishes*)
Yessum. Dey ain' no answeh.

75

PATRICIA

I saw Tommy, Ellen—about an hour ago.

ELLEN

Where?

PATRICIA

He was walking out on the little road back of the Ag buildings. Just moping along. I yelled at him, but he didn't hear me.

ELLEN

I'm getting worried.

JOE

(*Intent on his own activity*)

Everything's going to be okay. Nothing to worry about. . . . Now, study this play, girls, or you won't know it when you see it this afternoon. This is Michigan. And this is Midwestern. . . . Now! From the balanced line, we shift. Hup! (*He executes a Notre Dame shift, grimaces a little as his right knee resents this activity*) Wally takes the left-end's place, but he plays out a little.

(PATRICIA *exchanges cup and cream pitcher.*)

PATRICIA

Isn't Wally going to carry the ball?

JOE

Shh. Michigan spreads out. They're watching that wide end, but it's too obvious. They're watching the other side of the line, too.

76

GUERNSEY MEMORIAL
LIBRARY
NORWICH N Y

CLEOTA

(*Moving down, wide-eyed*)

What's goin' on heah?

ELLEN

Football game!

JOE

(*Ignoring her*)

The ball is snapped back. Now look, here we go! Both of us. . . . (*Carrying a plate and a napkin*) Close together. Fading back, but threatening a left-end run as well as a pass.

PATRICIA

But who are you?

JOE

I'm both of them—Lindstrom and Wierasocka . . . (*Comes forward*) Skolsky cuts down the left side line deep and takes out Wupperman—that's the jam pot. (*He picks up "Wally"*) Wally is running wide around right end (*Runs around end*) faking as though he had the ball but hasn't really got it— apparently! . . . Now, then, just as Michigan is charging in on Lindstrom and Wierasocka, trying to decide which one has the ball, Wally lets himself out! *He's really* got it!

PATRICIA

Hooray!

JOE

It's a fake fake. It's an old play, so corny only a football genius like Coach Sprague would use it. With no interference at all, Wally cuts over and goes straight down the right

77

side of the field! He stiff-arms the safety man ... (*Running with the cream pitcher*) Touchdown!

PATRICIA

Whoopee! (*She knocks over the jam pot*) Oh, God, there goes Wupperman!

(*During* JOE's *"touchdown,"* TOMMY *has appeared quietly in the door to the back yard. He watches* JOE *with distaste. No one notices him in the confusion.*)

CLEOTA

Um-hm. You through playin' now?

(PATRICIA *and* JOE *help her pick up the dishes.*)

PATRICIA

I'm sorry, Ellen.

ELLEN

It's all right. You can take the teams to the showers now, Cleota. Can't she, Joe?

JOE

Sure. How do you like it?

ELLEN

I think it's nice.

JOE

Nice?! It's marvelous! That play is going to put us in the Rose Bowl. (*To* PATRICIA) Did I ever tell you about how we used the Statue of Liberty play? (*He uses a cream pitcher as a football*) I would go back for a pass, and Jonesy would take it out of my hand and cut around to the left . . . (*He loses himself in the play, then suddenly realizes that not the imaginary ball but the cream pitcher has been taken out of his hand and that there is no Jonesy. He looks around slowly, puzzled, too late to have seen* TOMMY *quietly returning to the outdoors with the pitcher which he has snatched from* JOE's *hand. Doorbell rings.*)

ELLEN

I'll answer it. (*She goes to the front door.* JOE *looks to see where he might have dropped the pitcher; he is vastly puzzled.*)

PATRICIA

It's a wonderful play, Mr. Ferguson. If it works. (*She runs upstairs.*)

79

JOE

The coach gave it to me in strictest confidence. (*He gives another look for the pitcher with the expression of a prize bloodhound who has lost a scent.* ELLEN *admits* DEAN DAMON.)

ELLEN

Can you come in and wait, Dr. Damon? Tommy is out somewhere, but I'm expecting him back.

(CLEOTA *goes out with the tray and dishes, leaving the coffee things on a table.*)

DAMON

I can't wait very long. (*Indicates the magazine in his pocket.*)

ELLEN

Is that *The Literary Magazine?*

DAMON

It's a powder magazine. The bombs are bursting all around. (*He sees* JOE, *who has been putting on his coat and looking in the door drapes for the lost pitcher*) Oh—good afternoon.

JOE

How are you, Dr. Damon?

(*The phone rings.*)

ELLEN

Excuse me—I'll . . . (*She goes to the phone*) Hello. . . . Yes, thank you. That was Ed Keller's office, Joe. He's on his way over here.

JOE

Oh, yeah. He called me this morning. He's fit to be tied about this literary magazine thing. Have you seen it?

DAMON

Yes. This is it.

JOE

May I take a look at it? Gosh, I didn't realize what this thing was— (*He takes the magazine and scans the editorial*) Calls the trustees Fascists! This kid's dangerous—un-American.

DAMON

Oh, no.

ELLEN

Oh, no, not really. He's from an old Chillicothe family.

JOE

This is bad stuff for the university. I'm afraid all hell's going to break loose. Of course, it's none of my business, but . . .

DAMON

(*Taking the magazine out of* JOE's *hand*)
You take the words right out of my mouth. It's been a very trying morning. I haven't had such a day since poor Dr. Prendergast shot his secretary.

JOE

Well, I'm not a trustee, but I know how they feel.

ELLEN

(*Anxiously*)

I know.

JOE

Tommy'd better deny this, pretty fast, and get himself out in the clear, I'm telling you. I'm sorry about this, Ellen. Where is Tommy?

ELLEN

I don't know.

JOE

You don't think— (*He lowers his voice*) You don't think he may be a little sore about your going out with me last night?

ELLEN

I don't know. Oh, Joe, I'm all upset.
    (*The doorbell rings.*)

JOE

Shall I open it? (*He does*) Hi, Ed.

ED

(*Off-stage*)

Turner here?

ELLEN

No, he isn't.
    (ED *appears in the doorway.*)

ED

(*Sternly*)

Well, I want to see him before the game. Tell him to call my office. Coming, Joe?

ELLEN

(*Quickly*)

I don't know just when he'll . . . Won't you come in?
Dr. Damon is here.

ED

Oh. (*He comes into the room a few steps.* JOE *closes the
door*) Well, I'm glad somebody's here. How do you do, sir?
Do you know where I could find President Cartwright?

DAMON

His secretary informed me that he is at the barber shop
having his beard trimmed.

ED

(*His anger going up fast*)

That'll be a big help! I thought Turner was going to deny
this story. Papers keep calling *me*—they say he hasn't. Here
I am, bearing the brunt of this damn disgraceful attack.
"Fascists!" You oughtta heard Si McMillan! And do you
know Kressinger's in town from Detroit?

ELLEN

Is he a trustee, too?

DAMON

Oh, yes, young Michael has exploded his dynamite at a
moment when the concentration of trustees is at its thickest.

ED

Yeh. There goes the new stadium. There goes your Endowment Fund! Unless something is done, and done quick!
(*He turns on* ELLEN, *with a roar*) Ellen, you tell your husband
what I said!

83

JOE

(*Moving in*)

Look, Ed, it isn't Ellen's fault.

ED

(*Between fury and tears*)

It isn't my fault, either. I kept this whole week end free. I got my office full of eighteen-year-old Bourbon so we fellows could cut loose a little. And look what happens! All we need now is for Wierasocka to fumble a punt! (*He stomps out of the house.*)

JOE

I'll—see you later. (*He goes out after* ED.)

DAMON

I didn't like the way Mr. Keller said "There goes your Endowment Fund." (*The phone rings*) If that's the newspapers I'm not here.

ELLEN

Oh, I don't want to talk to them either. Cleota—

(*As the phone rings again,* PATRICIA *runs down the stairs.*)

PATRICIA

(*Angrily*)

I'm going out to talk to Michael! I got him on the phone but he hung up on me! Good afternoon, Dr. Damon. I'll knock his ears off. (*She slams out the door. The phone rings on.*)

DAMON

Good afternoon, Patricia.

(CLEOTA *enters from the dining room.*)

84

ELLEN

Answer the phone, Cleota.

CLEOTA

(*Picking up the receiver cautiously*)

Hello. . . . Says what? . . . Say, he *is*? . . . Ah didn' say you said he was, Ah say what is it? . . . No, he ain' heah. . . . No, dis ain' Miz Turner. (*She is getting a little surly.*)

ELLEN

Who is calling, please!

CLEOTA

Who's dis? . . . Wait a minute. . . . (*She puts her hand over the mouthpiece. To* ELLEN) It's de Daily sumpin'.

ELLEN

Hang up, Cleota.

CLEOTA

(*Brightly*)

G'bye. (*She hangs up and exits.*)

ELLEN

Oh, Lord, see what's happened already! Dr. Damon, suppose Tommy *didn't* read this letter?

DAMON

Let us not take refuge in conditional clauses.

ELLEN

Would *you* read it if you were Tommy?

85

DAMON

Now we go into the subjunctive. My dear, for forty-two years I have read nothing to *my* classes which was written later than the first half of the seventeenth century.

ELLEN

There must be some way—some compromise—that wouldn't be too humiliating.

DAMON

The policy of appeasement? Yes, it has its merits. (*He rises*) I can't wait any longer for Thomas. Tell him that if he decides not to read the letter, I shall feel easier in my mind. Much easier. (*He picks up his hat*) And—slightly disappointed. . . . Good afternoon, my dear. . . . (*He opens the door, and in flies* PATRICIA. *They collide*) Wup, wup, WUP!

PATRICIA

Don't let Michael in! I don't want to talk to him any more!

DAMON

Did you—uh—knock his ears off?

PATRICIA
(*Loudly*)

I got him told! But he wants to tell me *his* side. He thinks *he* has a side.

DAMON
(*Quietly*)

A common failing, my dear. . . . Good afternoon. (*He goes out and* PATRICIA *bolts the door after him, hotly.*)

PATRICIA

There, I've bolted that young genius out! Oh, Ellen! Give me a football player any time. (*She crosses to her sister for comfort*) Give me a guy without so much intellect or whatever it is. Somebody that doesn't want to be bawling the world out all the time—always doing something brave or fine or something. (MICHAEL, *greatly upset, steps into the room from the back yard*) Go away!

ELLEN

Quiet down, Patricia. . . . Come in, Michael.

MICHAEL

(*To* PATRICIA)

You're being very silly.

ELLEN

(*Noticing* MICHAEL's *distraught look*)

Can I give you a glass of milk?

MICHAEL

No, thank you. She won't listen to me, Mrs. Turner. I'm not trying to ruin your husband's life or my life or anybody's life. It's the principle of the thing she won't see.

PATRICIA

Oh, the principle! (*She stomps over to him*) I'll bet nobody else would make a fool of himself and his friends and—my brother-in-law—over a principle.

    (ELLEN, *taking the dishes with her, quietly slips out to the kitchen, unnoticed by* MICHAEL.)

87

MICHAEL

(*With the enormous gravity of the young man in love*)
All right, Pat. I'm very glad to know the qualities you admire in a man. They are certainly the noble virtues, and I'm sure Wally is lousy with them.

PATRICIA

Oh, make up your mind who you're imitating, Ralph Waldo Emerson or Hemingway! You—you *writer!*

MICHAEL

Now who's imitating Hemingway?

PATRICIA

I wish you'd go away!

MICHAEL

(*Rushing to the front door*)
I'm going! I'm going for good! I'm going out of your life!
(*On the last word he jerks at the door to make a dramatic exit, but it won't open, since* PATRICIA *bolted it. The doorknob comes off in his hand.*)

PATRICIA

(*Going out the lower door to the porch*)
It's bolted, you dope!
  (MICHAEL *gets the door open finally and in walks an extremely puzzled* TOMMY *with the other door-knob in his hand. The two stand and look at each other.*)

MICHAEL
(*A little guiltily*)

Sorry, Mr. Turner!

TOMMY

What's going on here?
(MICHAEL *puts his knob in and* TOMMY *screws the other knob on.*)

MICHAEL

I was just going.

TOMMY

That's all right. Come in, if you want to.

MICHAEL
(*Noticing* TOMMY'S *haggard look*)

Say, you look terrible.

TOMMY

Me? Why, what's the matter?

MICHAEL
(*His mind on his own woes*)

I've got to get out of here.

TOMMY

Why? Did somebody do something to you?

MICHAEL

Patricia. She did plenty. I suppose it's just as well. I've found out what she wants in life: a handsome, half-witted half-back.

TOMMY

Yes, I know how that feels.

MICHAEL

Yes, sir. Well, you can't get anywhere with a woman who doesn't understand what you have to do.

TOMMY

No. No, you can't, Michael. You'd like to, but you can't. . . . Good-bye, Michael. . . . (*He shakes hands with* MICHAEL, *grimly*) Come back in about an hour, will you? I want to give you a piece of my mind.

MICHAEL

(*Puzzled*)

Yes, sir. (*He goes slowly out the front door, as* TOMMY *takes the picture he snatched from* JOE *out of his overcoat pocket.* TOMMY *sits sadly, and sighs as* ELLEN *enters.*)

ELLEN

Oh, hello, darling!

TOMMY

Hello.

ELLEN

(*Uneasily*)

Well, I'm glad you remembered where you live. I was beginning to be worried. We phoned your office three times, but nobody knew where you were.

TOMMY

(*Looking up slowly*)

Huh?

ELLEN

I say nobody knew where you were—since early this morning.

TOMMY

I was walking.

ELLEN

Without any breakfast? All this time?

TOMMY

Well, I—came around to the back door a while ago, but Joe was doing the Statue of Liberty or something again, so I went away.

ELLEN

You were right here and you went away?

TOMMY

Yes, I couldn't face that right now. Not the Statue of Liberty.

ELLEN

Oh. Well, Dr. Damon's been here—and Ed Keller, and the newspapers have been calling up. There's going to be a lot of trouble if you don't hurry up and deny that story of Michael's—or have you done it?

TOMMY

No—I haven't denied it.

91

ELLEN

(*Troubled*)

You mean you've made up your mind to read it? Is that what you've been—walking around for? Tommy, I don't know what to say to you.

TOMMY

I think maybe you've said enough already.

ELLEN

That isn't very kind.

TOMMY

None of this is going to sound very kind but I've figured out exactly what I want to say, and I have to get it out before I get all mixed up.

ELLEN

I don't see why you are being so mean.

TOMMY

It's just that last night I began to see you, and myself, clearly for the first time.

ELLEN

If this is a story you're writing, and you're trying it out on me, it isn't very good.

TOMMY

Oh, I saw you and Joe clearly, too.

ELLEN

(*Relieved, crosses to* TOMMY)

Oh, you saw him kiss me. . . . I thought that was it. . . .

92

TOMMY

No. . . . No, I didn't. . . . Did he kiss you? Well, that's
fine. . . . I've been meaning to ask you, what became of
Housman's "Last Poems"? (*He turns to the bookshelves.*)

ELLEN

Tommy (*She puts her hand on his shoulder*), listen to me.
. . . I wanted to have a good time last night, and you spoiled
it. . . .

TOMMY

Didn't you enjoy it at all?

ELLEN

(*Piqued*)

Yes, I did. I'm not a hundred years old—yet. I just decided
to quit worrying about you and have a little fun. For about
an hour I felt like a girl again—wearing flowers at a Spring
dance—when I was young and silly. . . .

TOMMY

Young and happy.

ELLEN

All right, he . . . kissed me. I kissed him, too. We didn't
go out in the dark to do it.

TOMMY

(*Piling the books he is taking from the bookshelves on
the settee*)

I hope you didn't lend that book to anybody; it was a first
edition.

ELLEN

Did you *hear* what I *said?*

TOMMY

Sure, I heard you. I'm listening. . . . You said you went out in the dark and kissed Joe.

ELLEN

I said no such thing! and you know it.

TOMMY

I wish we had had separate bookplates.

ELLEN

(*Beginning to flame*)

So that when you really make me mad and I get out of here, I can find my own books quickly?

TOMMY

I hate sentimental pawing over things by a couple breaking up. We're not living in the days of Henry James and Meredith. Look at Joe and his wife.

ELLEN

Tommy. (*She goes to him again*) I want you to stop this. If you're going to be jealous *be* jealous, rave or throw things, but don't act like the lead in a senior-class play! (*This thrust gets home.*)

TOMMY

(*Angrily*)

I'm trying to tell you that I don't care what you and Joe

do! I'm trying to tell you that it's fine! It's very lucky that he came back just now.

ELLEN

Why, what do you mean?

TOMMY

I mean on the money *I* make, I can go on fine alone, reading whatever I want to to my classes! That's what I want! And that's what I'm going to do.

ELLEN

Oh, that's what you want! Suddenly that's what you want. More than me?

TOMMY

It isn't so sudden. Not any more sudden than your feeling for Joe. It's logical. We get in each other's way. You wear yourself out picking up after me. Taking matches out of my pockets. Disarranging my whole way of life. (*She follows him as he moves away from her.*)

ELLEN

Why haven't you said all this before?

TOMMY

I couldn't very well.

ELLEN

Why couldn't you? If you felt this way?

TOMMY

Well, we hadn't split up on this letter issue, for one thing— and then there was no place for you to go. (*He sits on a sofa*) I didn't want you to have to go back to Cleveland, or to work in some tea shoppe!

ELLEN

Oh, I see. Some tea shoppe! That's what you think I'd have to do! Well, you needn't have spared my feelings. I can make as much money as you!

TOMMY

You don't have to, now.

ELLEN

(*Whirling*)

Oh, you mean you waited to tell me all this till Joe came along! I thought you were jealous of Joe. I could understand that. You aren't the least bit aroused at the idea of his kissing me—*out in the dark—for hours!*

TOMMY

No, I'm not.

ELLEN

(*Full of exclamation points*)

So that's why you've been wandering around! That's what you've been figuring out! How nice it would be if he would take me off your hands, so you could be left alone with your books and match boxes and *litter!* I suppose any man would do as well as Joe! (*She rushes up to him.*)

TOMMY

(*Rising to face her*)

He's not just any man, and you know that! He's always

96

been in love with you, and you've always been in love with him! (*He is angry and jealous now and brings up his own exclamation points.*)

ELLEN

That's ridiculous!

TOMMY

(*Moving toward her*)

I felt it when I saw you dancing together. It was unmistakable. You've just admitted it.

ELLEN

Oh, you can't do that *now!* You can't be jealous *now,* just because you think I want you to be!

TOMMY

(*Rising to his big denunciation*)

I saw you dancing together—like angels! I saw you go out in that goddamn carriage together! I saw you together years ago, when I was young enough and dumb enough to believe that I really took you away from him. There's something that happens when you two dance together that doesn't happen when *we* dance together!

ELLEN

(*Worried, angry and tired*)

All right—have it your way. If you want to be free, then I want to be free—and I've gone around for ten years mooning about Joe. . . . Well, maybe I have—maybe I have, because I'm certainly sick of you right now! (*She whirls away from him.*)

97

TOMMY

(*Deathly afraid of her being sick of him*)
Ellen . . . Ellen, listen!

ELLEN

Never mind—all right—*all right*— ALL RIGHT! (*She is shouting as* JOE *enters brightly.*)

JOE

Oh, I'm sorry—if I . . . (*He stops in embarrassment. There is a pause. He has caught only the tone; but he sees and feels the tension. He is carrying a wrapped bottle and a newspaper.*)

TOMMY

Hello, Joe.

JOE

Hello. I brought the rum. (*He crosses to the coffee table, puts the bottle on the table; holds up the newspaper*) Big picture of Wally all over the front page. (ELLEN *stares out the window,* TOMMY *stares at* JOE) Good picture, isn't it?

TOMMY

You and Ellen have some rum.

JOE

The rum's for the punch—later.

ELLEN

Could I have some—now?
(TOMMY *goes out to dining room.*)

98

JOE
(*Surprised*)

Right now? Sure.

TOMMY
(*Yelling from dining room*)

I'll get you some glasses. (*He reappears with two glasses.*)

JOE
(*Unscrewing the top of the rum bottle*)

Tommy, old man, I just left Ed Keller and Si McMillan. This thing your young friend wrote in the magazine. (*Pours a drink*) I read that piece over again. He's got you on a spot, Tommy. (*He gives* ELLEN *her drink.*)

ELLEN

Want to drink a toast, Joe? To Tommy's happiness?
(JOE *looks at both of them.*)

JOE
(*Puzzled*)

Sure. . . . (*Pours himself a drink*) Your happiness, Tommy. (*They drink amid a long silence,* JOE *nervously finishing his,* ELLEN *taking a long drink, grimacing as it burns her throat.* JOE *decides to dive in*) What's the matter? What's it about? Maybe I could talk to Ed . . .

TOMMY

No. I don't want that. I'll run my own life my own way.

ELLEN

That's what it's about. Tommy wants to—live alone.

99

JOE

What?

ELLEN

He wants to be left alone. . . .

JOE

I beg your pardon?

ELLEN
(*Almost shouting*)
Us! Tommy and me! We're breaking up!

JOE
(*Awed*)
Just before the game? You're both crazy! Maybe I better go.

TOMMY

Not at all. You're not exactly a stranger around here. You knew Ellen as long ago as I did.

JOE

I knew her a long time before you did . . . and this is a hell of a way to be treating her.

TOMMY
(*Baiting a hook*)
Yes, I know. I was just saying I barged in and took her away from you.

(ELLEN *stares at* TOMMY.)

JOE

(*Taking the bait*)

Oh, no, you didn't! You had nothing to do with it. She got sore at me on account of another girl.

TOMMY

(*Triumphantly*)

Oh, *that's* where I came in?

JOE

Sure. If you think you took her away from me, you're crazy. Here, you better have some rum.

ELLEN

(*The wife*)

He can't drink this early.

TOMMY

I don't *need* any rum. Go on, Joe.

JOE

(*Sitting near* TOMMY)

Well, Ellen and I had a fight. You weren't in on it. You came in later. . . .

ELLEN

(*Wearily, also warily*)

Joe, do we have to . . .

TOMMY

It's all right. It's his turn.

JOE

She said she hated me and never wanted to see me again. She threw something at me. She thought I slept with this girl—I mean . . .

TOMMY

(*Coolly*)

I know what you mean. . . .

ELLEN

(*Indignantly*)

I never said you sl . . . I never said that.

JOE

(*Turning from* TOMMY *to* ELLEN)

Oh, yes, you did—you intimated it.

ELLEN

No, that was *your* idea. I thought you were bragging about it!

JOE

(*Turning farther away from* TOMMY)

Well, you got awfully mad. I thought you never did want to see me again. I guess I was dumb. Brenda says it shows you liked me. (*From* ELLEN's *expression,* JOE *is reminded of* TOMMY's *presence. He turns to* TOMMY, *a little sheepishly*) Oh—sorry.

TOMMY

(*The tolerant man of the world*)

Oh, don't mind me. Who's Brenda? Another girl?

102

JOE

My wife.

TOMMY

Oh, sorry.

JOE

Ellen knows her. She's from Cleveland. Brenda's always been jealous of Ellen. She found a picture of you.

TOMMY

(*Not so tolerant*)

What picture?

ELLEN

I gave him a picture. He wouldn't give it back.

JOE

It's a swell picture. You were wearing that floppy hat. Red.

ELLEN

Blue.

JOE

It had ribbons. Made you look like you were sixteen.

TOMMY

I've never seen it.

ELLEN

It was a silly hat. This was ages ago.

TOMMY

I mean, I've never seen the picture.

103

ELLEN

(*Angrily*)

I threw them all away.

JOE

(*Looking back over the years*)

It kind of went down over one eye.

TOMMY

(*Remembering an old lovely hat*)

She looks nice in hats like that.

(ELLEN *suddenly begins to cry and collapses on the sofa.*)

JOE

(*Rising*)

Now look what you've done!

TOMMY

(*Rising*)

Look what *you've* done! Bringing up old floppy blue hats! (JOE *moves to* ELLEN) Don't touch her! She doesn't like to be touched when she's crying.

JOE

I've seen her cry. I know what to do.

TOMMY

Oh, you do?

JOE

She cried when we had that fight about the girl. She was lying on the floor and crying and kicking—on her stomach.

104

ELLEN

I was not!

TOMMY

Be careful what you say!

JOE

Well, I mean I knew what to do. (*Crosses to other end of sofa*) I picked her up that time.

TOMMY
(*Following him*)
Well, you're not going to pick her up now.

ELLEN

Will you both please let me alone?! Will you please go away!

JOE
(*Getting sore*)
She wants you to go away. And I don't blame her, if this is the way you treat her. I wouldn't have stood for it ten years ago, and I'm not going to stand for it now.

TOMMY

But what are you going to do?

JOE

I'm going to get her away from all this! It isn't *nice!*

TOMMY

It isn't exactly to my taste, either. I didn't want it to turn

105

out this way, but it did. Ellen crying, me feeling like a cad, and you acting like a fool.

JOE

Me acting like a fool?

ELLEN

(*Sitting up*)

Everybody's acting like a fool.

JOE

You've certainly messed things up, brother.

TOMMY

Don't call me brother! I can't stand that now.

JOE

If Ellen weren't here, I'd call you worse than brother!

ELLEN

Well, I'm not going to be here! Please, please stop—both of you! Nobody has said a word about what I want to do. You're going to settle that between yourselves. Bandying me back and forth!

TOMMY

Nobody's bandying you, Ellen.

ELLEN

(*Mad*)

I know when I'm being bandied! (*On her feet*) I don't want either of you! You can both go to hell! (*She runs upstairs, crying.*)

(*Both men follow and look after her*)

TOMMY

She means me.

JOE

She said both of us.

TOMMY

She was looking at me.

JOE

How did we get into this, anyway?

TOMMY

You two-stepped into it. You kissed your way into it.

JOE

I'm sorry about that. Sorry it happened.

TOMMY

You're not sorry it happened. You're sorry I found it out. Do you know anything about women? Didn't you know what she was thinking about when she was dancing with you?

JOE

No. I don't think when I'm dancing.

TOMMY

I know. You think in your office. Well, you'll have to think in your home after this. She likes to be thought about.

JOE

I thought about her. I remembered her birthday. I brought her flowers.

TOMMY

Well, you'll have to keep on bringing her things whether it's her birthday or not. Fur coats and—things. She's still young and pretty.

JOE

(*Narrowing his eyes*)

I don't get you.

TOMMY

I'm being broadminded. I'm taking things in my stride. It's the modern way of doing things. You ought to know that.

JOE

(*Shrewdly*)

Um, hm. But what makes me think you're still crazy about her and are up to some goddamn something or other?

108

TOMMY

(*A little taken aback*)

Don't be acute. I couldn't stand you being acute.

JOE

I'm not dumb.

TOMMY

Yes, you are. It isn't what *I* feel that counts. It's what *she* feels. I think she's always been in love with you. Why, I don't know. It's supposed to be beyond reason. I guess it is.

JOE

You think that just because of last night?

TOMMY

No. Because of what lay behind last night. That wasn't just a kiss. That's nothing. This thing is too deep for jealousy or for anything but honesty. A woman must not go on living with a man when she dances better with another man.

JOE

That's silly! *That's the silliest* . . . ! Dancing doesn't mean everything!

TOMMY

The way *you* do it does. The thing that happens to you. The *light* you give off.

JOE

Light?!

109

TOMMY

Oh, these things are too subtle for you, Joe. I've made some study of them. (*Turns away.*)

JOE

Maybe all this studying's bad for you.

TOMMY

(*Pinning him down*)

All I want to know is whether you felt the same thing she felt last night.

JOE

I felt fine. This is goddamn embarrassing! A man makes love to a woman. He doesn't talk it over with her husband!

TOMMY

I'm just trying to be honest.

JOE

You're a funny guy. Conscientious. What does it get you? Like this letter you're going to read. . . . Say, is that what started the trouble?

TOMMY

Yes, it's an integral part of the trouble—things like that.

JOE

Well, what are we going to do? I mean now? I mean from now on?

TOMMY

From now on will work itself out. Right now you'd better go upstairs and comfort her. She'll be expecting you.

JOE

Oh, no. Not me! You ought to know more what to do right now. It's your house. She's your wife.

TOMMY

She doesn't want to talk to me. She's just done that. But she oughtn't to be left alone right now.

JOE
(*Rises*)
Well— (*He takes a few steps*) What'll I say?

TOMMY

What did you say last night, when you were dancing?

JOE
(*Going to the foot of the stairs*)
It doesn't seem right somehow for me to go upstairs.

TOMMY

This is not a moment for cheap moralizing!

JOE

Well—good God almighty! (*He goes upstairs.*)
     (MICHAEL *has come in the front door in time to hear*
     JOE's *last expletive.*)

MICHAEL
(*As* TOMMY *looks after* JOE)
What's the matter?

111

TOMMY

Never mind. . . . (*He paces, glares upstairs, still has his glare when he turns back to* MICHAEL.)

MICHAEL

Well, I came back like you said. Before you start in on me, Mr. Turner, please remember that I've been through a lot today. I can't stand much more. (TOMMY *pats him on shoulder. Gloomily*) They'll probably do something to you—especially if we lose to Michigan. You know what Keller did the last time they beat us in a Homecoming Game? He ran the flag on his office building down to half-mast.

TOMMY

(*Looking upstairs—distracted*)

Don't worry about me.

MICHAEL

Well, I'm feeling better. I've put her out of my mind. It's ended as simply as that. (*He drops into a chair*) There's a girl who could sit with you and talk about Shelley. Well, I'm glad I found out about women. (*Crash upstairs*) What was that?

TOMMY

I'm sure I don't know. What were you saying?

MICHAEL

I say Patricia knew things. She knew odd things like "A Sonnet on Political Greatness." She quoted that one night. Wouldn't you think a girl like that had some social consciousness?

112

TOMMY

That's the sonnet that ends:
> "Quelling the anarchy of hopes and fears,
> Being himself alone."

MICHAEL

Yes, but when an issue comes up and a man has to be himself alone, she reveals the true stature of her character and goes off to Hennick's with that football player. I saw them—right in the front window—drinking Seven-Up. He uses a straw.

TOMMY

Yes, but he's handsome. What is more, he whirls. He's a hunter. He comes home at night with meat slung over his shoulders, and you sit there drawing pictures on the wall of your cave.

MICHAEL

I see. Maybe I ought to sock him with a ball-bat.

TOMMY

No. You are a civilized man, Michael. If the male animal in you doesn't like the full implications of that, he must nevertheless be swayed by Reason. You are not living in the days of King Arthur when you fought for your woman. Nowadays, the man and his wife and the other man talk it over. Quietly and calmly. They all go out to dinner together. (*He sits on the sofa across the stage from* MICHAEL.)

MICHAEL

Intellectually, Patricia is sleeping with that guy. I feel like going out tonight with the Hot Garters.

TOMMY

With the what?

MICHAEL

It's a girl. They call her that. What if she was kicked out of the Pi Phi House? She's honest! She does what she believes in! And—well, Hot Garters doesn't argue all the time anyway.

TOMMY
(*Removing his glasses*)

Look, hasn't she got a name? You don't call her *that,* do you?

MICHAEL

Marcia Gardner. They just call her . . .

TOMMY

Yes, you told me what they call her.
(*Slight pause.*)

MICHAEL

Patricia's not coming to class when you read that letter. She's gone over to the Philistines. . . . Oh, God, Mr. Turner, I wish I were like you! Middle-aged, settled down, happily married—and through with all this hell you feel when you're young and in love.

TOMMY
(*Nettled*)

Middle-aged?

MICHAEL

Yes, you know what Rupert Brooke says:

114

"That time when all is over. . . .
        (TOMMY *writhes, turns his back*)
            And love has turned to kindliness."
Is kindliness peaceful?

TOMMY

Don't ask *me*. (*Two quick crashes from upstairs bring* TOMMY *to his feet just as* JOE *hurries down the stairs, looking worn and worried, his hair slightly disarranged. Sharply*) You look ruffled!

JOE
(*Just as sharply, but a bit absently*)
What? (*The two men look each other over.*)

TOMMY

I say—what ruffled you?

JOE

Do we have to discuss these things in front of this boy?

MICHAEL
(*Rising*)

I am not a boy.

TOMMY

This is Michael Barnes.

JOE

Oh, so you're the little boy that started all this! I want to tell you that you write too much, you have too much to say, you get too many people into too much trouble. You've not only got Tommy and Ellen involved, but me.

MICHAEL

I don't see how this concerns you, do you, Mr. Turner?

TOMMY

Yes.

MICHAEL

Oh, well, I'll go out and climb a tree, Mr. Turner. I'll come back when this blows over. (*Goes out into the garden.*)

JOE

Oh, God, I wish I was in Pittsburgh! (*He sits heavily in chair vacated by* MICHAEL.)

TOMMY
(*Eagerly*)

What happened?

JOE

Well, old man, I guess you're right. She was pretty bitter—about you. She picked up something you'd given her and threw it against the wall and broke it into a thousand pieces.

TOMMY

What was it?

JOE

I didn't see it till after she threw it.

TOMMY

Oh.

JOE

Every time she mentioned your name, she threw something. Kept me ducking.

116

TOMMY
(*Sadly*)

I see. (*He, too, sits heavily on the large sofa*) You want to marry Ellen, don't you?

JOE

Well, I always liked her, but I don't like to go through so much. (*Pause*) Are you sure you understand women?

TOMMY

Yes.

JOE

Well, when Ellen and I had that fight about the girl, she threw things on account of me, and Brenda thinks that meant she was in love with me. Now she throws things on account of *you*.

TOMMY
(*After an instant of hope*)

In both instances, she threw them at *you*, didn't she?

JOE
(*Glumly*)

Yeh, I guess so.

TOMMY

Well, there you are. What did she say when you left? What was she doing?

JOE

She was in a terrible state. I don't think she'll be able to go to the game. She may have a sick headache for days. What do you do then?

TOMMY

(*Rises, and goes to dining room with sudden efficiency*)
You get her a hot-water bottle. Cleota! Cleota!

CLEOTA
(*Off-stage*)

Yes, suh?

TOMMY
(*Off-stage*)

There's a hot-water bottle out there in the . . . somewhere.
Fill it and bring it in, please.

CLEOTA
(*Off-stage*)

Yes, *suh*.

(TOMMY *returns.* JOE *glances at his wrist watch, rises,
and paces across stage.*)

JOE

I don't want to miss this game. I sort of wish Stalenkiwiecz
wasn't laid up, don't you?

TOMMY

(*Sits on sofa again*)
I haven't given it much thought one way or another.

JOE

Of course, Wierasocka's all right, but Stalenkiwiecz is a
better pass receiver.

118

TOMMY

Is he? Why?

JOE

I don't know why. He just is. "Why!" (*His pacing has carried him to the door leading to the garden. He remembers the vanishing pitcher and takes one more look, then resumes his prowl*) 'Course they may not give Brenda a divorce.

TOMMY

I think they will.

JOE

I don't know.
> (CLEOTA *comes in with hot-water bottle and towel. She hands them to* TOMMY.)

CLEOTA

Is you gotta pain?

TOMMY

No. Oh, thank you.
> (CLEOTA *retires.*)

JOE

I don't suppose we ought to go and leave her.

TOMMY
(*Going to him with bottle*)
Oh, I'm not going. Here. (*Hands him bottle and towel.*)

JOE
(*Taking it as if it were a baby*)
Ow!

TOMMY

Hold it by the end.

JOE

Won't this thing burn her?

TOMMY

(*Impatiently, showing him*)

You wrap the towel around it.

JOE

You shouldn't stay here in the house alone with her, things being the way they are, should you?

TOMMY

(*Turning away*)

Please don't worry about that!

JOE

(*Looking at the bottle*)

I thought these things were different now than they used to be.

TOMMY

What do you mean, different?

JOE

I mean better looking . . . somehow. (*There is a pause during which* JOE *tries to wrap the towel around the hot-*

water bottle, but various parts of it insist on remaining exposed. Finally TOMMY *crosses down to* JOE *angrily.*)

TOMMY

Well, why don't you take it up to her?

ELLEN

(*Coming down the stairs*)

It's time to get started, isn't it? (*The two men turn and stare at her,* JOE *still holding the hot-water bottle.* ELLEN *is utterly serene, with no sign of tears or hysterics. Washed and powdered, with her hat on, she stands at the foot of the stairs, ready for the game*) Do you realize what time it is? The Kellers will be waiting for us at Esther Baker's. We'll leave the car there and walk to the stadium. It's only a block. (*The men are still staring*) What are you doing with that thing, Joe?

TOMMY

He was going to lie down with it for a while.

JOE

I was not! Here! (*Tries to hand it to* TOMMY.)

TOMMY

I don't want it.

ELLEN

We've got to hurry, Joe. (*Takes the bottle from* JOE *and puts it on the sofa*) Have you got the tickets?

JOE

Yeh, I've got them. (*Goes to radio*) Say, what number is the game on?

ELLEN

It's around 1210 on the dial. (*As* JOE *turns on radio and fiddles with dial,* ELLEN *turns to* TOMMY) Sure you won't go to the game?

TOMMY

Oh, no. . . . (*With shy politeness*) How are you?

ELLEN

(*As if surprised at the question*)

Me? I'm fine.

(*As* JOE *keeps fiddling with dials, dance music comes on, then band music.*)

TOMMY

That's good.

JOE

Well, it hasn't started yet—just music. Let's go. (*Gets* ELLEN's *coat from hook*) This yours?

ELLEN

Yes.

JOE

Well, is it warm enough?

122

ELLEN

Yes. Oh, it's very warm.

TOMMY
(*Angrily*)

No, it isn't.
  (CLEOTA *enters with the thermos, which she gives to*
  TOMMY.)

CLEOTA

Here's your thermos, Mr. Turner.

TOMMY

Thank you. (*Takes it.* CLEOTA *goes out.*)

ELLEN

It's a very warm day, anyway, and we'll have the lap robe
from the car.

TOMMY

Ellen. (*She goes to him eagerly*) You forgot your thermos
bottle. . . . (*His tone is jocular, and he pretends to screw the
cap on tighter to cover his hurt*) You'd better make a note
of this, Joe. It gets cold in stadiums late in the afternoon.
Ellen gets chilly sometimes, so she likes hot coffee. . . . Well,
here. (*He hands thermos to* ELLEN. JOE *nods, goes to the front
door, and opens it.* ELLEN, *who has been staring at* TOMMY,
*suddenly throws the thermos bottle on the floor, then rushes
out, passing* JOE. JOE *looks after her, then comes back to face*
TOMMY *threateningly.*)

JOE

Did you slap her?

TOMMY

No, I kicked her.

JOE

Well, you did something!

(*An* ANNOUNCER'S VOICE *breaks into the band music.*)

JOE

(*Torn between interest in the announcement and his aroused chivalry*)

Here I get her all calmed down and you make her cry again. I see now what kind of a life she has here. I'm going to take her away from this and keep her away!

ANNOUNCER'S VOICE

Well, here we are on Midwestern's field on a mighty fine afternoon for a football game. . . . It looks like the Big Day of the year, folks. Neither one of these great teams has lost a game. The Michigan squad is out on the field warming up. They look even bigger than last year. . . .

TOMMY

(*Shouting*)

All right! Why don't you get started?

JOE

(*Topping him*)

Because I've got a few more things to say to you. First! (*As he takes a breath, the* ANNOUNCER'S VOICE *comes through clearly.*)

ANNOUNCER'S VOICE

Here comes the Scarlet Stampede now! (*There is a roar of cheering.*)

JOE

My God, they're coming out on the field! We'll miss the kick-off! *God damn it!!* (*He turns and dashes out the front door.* TOMMY *stands looking after him as the band blares, and the*

Curtain Falls

125

ACT TWO

Scene II

The Turner living room, two hours later. It is growing dark outside.

TOMMY *and* MICHAEL *are sitting in chairs wide apart, facing the audience, so that they have to turn their heads to see each other. Each has a glass in his hand, and they are sprawled in their chairs, silent, brooding. The room shows indications of quite a bout: a bottle here, a few magazines flung there, a cushion on the floor.* TOMMY *gets the Scotch bottle, pours a little into* MICHAEL'S *glass, emptying the bottle. He starts to pour some into his own glass, finds the bottle empty so pours some from* MICHAEL'S *glass into his own. Throws the bottle into the wastebasket. There is a pause.*

MICHAEL

He is probably still running with that ball. . . .
   (*Pause.*)

TOMMY

Quiet—quiet! . . . What time is it?

MICHAEL

   (*Looks at his wrist watch, has trouble seeing it*)
It's getting dark.
   (*Pause.*)

TOMMY

Do you know the first law of human nature?

MICHAEL

Yes. Self-propagation.

TOMMY

Not any more. That's gone with last year's nightingale.

MICHAEL

Gone with last year's rose.
(*Slight pause.*)

TOMMY

Yes. . . . Defense of the home. . . . Against prowlers and predatory—prowlers. . . . Do you know what the tiger does when the sanctity of his home is jeopardized?

MICHAEL

I know. You told me. He talks it over with the other man, quietly and calmly.

TOMMY

He does not. I'm ashamed of you.

MICHAEL

I think we must have another drink—possibly.

TOMMY

All right. Hey! HEY! (*He is pleased with this shouting*) That's the way to talk to 'em. (*He puts back his head and yells*) HEYYY!!
(CLEOTA *enters, and turns on the lights.*)

127

THE MALE ANIMAL

CLEOTA

Mistah Turner, what is it?

TOMMY

What do you want? Oh, we should like to have something more to drink.

CLEOTA

They ain' any more to drink. I'll make you some black coffee. (*She goes out.*)

TOMMY
(*Pause*)

What'd she say?

MICHAEL

Nothing.

TOMMY

Where was I?

MICHAEL

Let's see—you were talking about tigers.

TOMMY

Oh, yes. But let us take the wolf. What does he do? I mean, when they come for his mate. He tears 'em to pieces.

MICHAEL

But we are civilized men. Aren't we?

TOMMY

And so does the leopard, and the lion, and the hawk. They tear 'em to pieces. Without a word.

128

MICHAEL

You had it figured out the other way around a while ago. You said we should give up our women. (TOMMY *stands, falters*) It's better sitting down. (TOMMY *sits.*)

TOMMY

Let us say that the tiger wakes up one morning and finds that the wolf has come down on the fold. What does he—? Before I tell you what he does, I will tell you what he does not do.

MICHAEL

Yes, sir.

TOMMY

He does not expose everyone to a humiliating intellectual analysis. He comes out of his corner like this— (*Rises, assuming an awkward fighting pose, fists up, then sits quickly again*) The bull elephant in him is aroused.

MICHAEL

(*Plaintively*)

Can't you stick to one animal?

TOMMY

No, that's my point. All animals are the same, including the human being. We are male animals, too. (MICHAEL *stares at him, bewildered.*)

MICHAEL

You said . . .

TOMMY

Even the penguin. (*His voice shows some emotion as he*

thinks of the penguin) He stands for no monkey-business where his mate is concerned. Swans have been known to drown scotties who threatened their nests.

MICHAEL

I don't think so.

TOMMY

There it is, in us always, though it may be asleep. The male animal. The mate. When you are married long enough, you become a mate. . . . Think of the sea-lion for a minute.

MICHAEL

All right.

TOMMY

His mate is lying there in a corner of the cave on a bed of tender boughs or something. (*Turns to* MICHAEL *for confirmation*) Is that all right, "tender boughs"?

MICHAEL

Yeah!

TOMMY

(*Illustrating by a gesture, a great seal, or eel*)
Now, who comes swimming quietly in through the early morning mist, sleek and powerful, dancing and whirling and throwing kisses?

MICHAEL

Joe Ferguson.

TOMMY

And what do I do?

130

MICHAEL

You say, "Hello."

TOMMY

(*In self-disgust*)

The sea-lion knows better. He snarls. He gores. He roars with his antlers. He knows that love is a thing you do something about. He knows it is a thing that words can kill. You do something. You don't just sit there. (MICHAEL *rises*) I don't mean you. (MICHAEL *sits*) A woman likes a man who does something. All the male animals fight for the female, from the land crab to the bird of paradise. They don't just sit and talk. They act. (*He removes his glasses and blinks owlishly around*) I hope I have made all this clear to you. Are there any questions?

MICHAEL

No, sir.

(ELLEN *and* JOE *enter.* ELLEN *takes in the disordered room, the bottles on the floor,* TOMMY's *and* MICHAEL's *condition.* MICHAEL *and* TOMMY *rise.*)

ELLEN

Tommy! What in the world have you been doing?

TOMMY

Drinking.

ELLEN

What for?

TOMMY

I was celebrating. Ellen, I have found myself. (*Glances at* JOE) I know now what I have to do.

ELLEN

Yes, I know. We've been through all that.

TOMMY

Perhaps you had better go away for a little while. (*Waves toward stairs.*)

ELLEN

I'm going. I'll be down in a minute, Joe. (*She slams upstairs.*)

JOE

Boy, wasn't that some football game? I'm running Wally Myers for President.

TOMMY
(*Beckoning to* MICHAEL)

Come on. (*With drunken carefulness, he and* MIKE *begin moving furniture to the sides of the room.*)

JOE
(*Watches, slightly puzzled, making talk*)

Yes, sir, some game, wasn't it? What did you think of Michigan going into the lead like that? If Wally hadn't snared that pass . . .

MICHAEL

We didn't listen to the game.

JOE

You didn't listen to the game?

MICHAEL

No, we turned it off. (*He flips off an imaginary dial.*)

TOMMY

The game didn't last all this time. Where have you been?

JOE

Well, we stopped in at President Cartwright's house.

133

TOMMY

What for?

JOE

'Cause Ellen and I were making one last effort to get you out of this mess.

TOMMY

Ellen and you. You would know exactly what to do, wouldn't you?

JOE

You guys are pie-eyed!

TOMMY

(*To* MICHAEL)

Did you hear that?

MICHAEL

Yes.

JOE

What's the idea of moving all the furniture around like this?

TOMMY

I don't want you to break anything when you fall.

JOE

I'm not going to fall.

TOMMY

Yes, you are. I am going to knock you cold. (*The furniture safe,* TOMMY *rolls up his sleeves, and* MICHAEL *sits on the arm of a settee, watching.*)

JOE

(*Kindly*)

Let's sit down and talk this over.

134

TOMMY

(*Turning to* MICHAEL)

Talk, he says, to a man of action. Sit down, he says, to a tigress and her cubs!

JOE

How the hell did you guys get so cockeyed? I wish Ellen'd hurry up. (*Goes to dining-room door*) Cleota!

TOMMY

Don't call for help. I could take Cleota and you in the same ring!

JOE

Well, what's this all about?

TOMMY

You crept into this house to take Ellen away, didn't you? You thought it was the house of a professor who would talk and *talk* and TALK . . .

JOE

And by God you have! I came here to see a football game—

MICHAEL

That's a lie.

JOE

Why don't you go home?

MICHAEL

'Cause I want to watch.

JOE

Well, there isn't going to be anything to watch.

135

TOMMY
(*Assuming a fighter's pose*)
Come on, put up your fists.

JOE
Get away from me, Tommy. (*Pushes* TOMMY's *arm which pivots* TOMMY *around so he faces* MICHAEL) I'd break you in two, and I don't want to do that.

TOMMY
(*Speaking first to* MIKE, *then, realizing he is facing the wrong way, turning to* JOE)
Why don't you want to do that?

JOE
'Cause how would it look if I came here and took Ellen and knocked you down on the way out?

MICHAEL
Maybe he's right. That's a point of honor, Mr. Turner.

TOMMY
Is it?

MICHAEL
But we could fight him about something else.

TOMMY
About what?

MICHAEL
He doesn't want you to read that letter.

TOMMY

That's right. (MICHAEL *rises and slowly moves to a spot behind* JOE) Going to the president's office. Trying to make me lose my job.

JOE

Why the hell should I?

TOMMY

So you could get Ellen.

JOE

Now, listen—

TOMMY

Yes! Now I'm going to have to knock you further than I had previously decided upon. Come out in the back yard. (*He tugs at* JOE, *but doesn't move him.* MICHAEL *helpfully gives* JOE *a good push.*)

JOE

(*Turns and strides back to* MICHAEL)

Don't push me!

TOMMY

Hey! (*As* JOE *turns,* TOMMY *lunges at* JOE *with a badly aimed haymaker.* JOE *ducks and catches* TOMMY *to keep him from falling.*)

JOE

Now look, if you do ever get in a fight, Tommy, don't lead with your right. It leaves you wide open.

TOMMY

Oh, does it?

(ELLEN *comes down the stairs with a suitcase which*

137

she drops when she sees the odd positions of the belligerents.)

ELLEN

What's happened? Tommy, what are you doing now?

TOMMY

Fighting.
> (*The music of the band is heard in the distance. Through the following scene it grows louder to* ELLEN's *exit, then dies away as the band goes around the corner, and comes up again for the end of the scene.*)

ELLEN
(Hopefully)

Fighting! What about?

MICHAEL

Penguins.

ELLEN

What!

JOE
(Trying to explain)

Oh, it was all mixed up—about that letter thing and a lot of tigers and a cub. Tommy doesn't care what you and I are trying to do! He wants us to stay out of it!

ELLEN
(Disappointed bitterly)

Oh, I see. That's what you were fighting about.

138

TOMMY

It wasn't about you. Point of honor.

ELLEN

Oh, yes, I see. You don't want me mixed up in anything. All right. You can pull the house down on top of you with your damn birds and letters and whiskey. Just let me get out of—what is all that racket!!

JOE

(*Opens the door a crack, then closes it*)
Oh, they're having a victory parade, and they want me to ride in that damn carriage with Wally Myers and the band.

TOMMY

You attract bands like flies, don't you?

ELLEN

(*As she starts for the door*)
Good-bye, Tommy! I'll be out in the car, Joe! Bring my bag, please! (*She slams out. The men look after her; then* JOE *gets* ELLEN's *bag, and faces* TOMMY.)

JOE

You're getting me in deeper and deeper! I shoulda taken a poke at you when I had the chance!

TOMMY

Fine! Come out in the back yard! (*He walks to the garden door, holds it open.*)

139

JOE

I'm not coming out in the back yard! (MICHAEL *pushes him, and* TOMMY, *catching him, turns him around to the lower door*) Don't push me. I said, I don't like to be pushed!

TOMMY

No . . . You said, "Don't lead with your right." (*He hits* JOE *on the nose with his* left *hand*.)

JOE

(*Pinching bridge of nose*)

Ow-w-w! Now you've started my sinus trouble! (*He flings down suitcase and spreads his hand easily across* TOMMY's *face*) By God, if you want a fight, you've got a fight! (*He pushes* TOMMY *outside, his arms flailing the air*.)

> (MICHAEL *plants a chair in front of the door and sits watching the fight off-stage. He applauds its progress*.)

MICHAEL

Hit him! Hit him! (*Quotes softly:*)

> "And all the summer afternoon
> They hunted us and slew!
> But tomorrow—by the living God!
> We'll try the game again!"

Don't forget to lead with your right, Mr. Turner! . . . That's right! Right in the eye!

> (CLEOTA *is attracted from the dining room by the noise.* WALLY *and* PATRICIA *come in the front door, rush over to* MICHAEL, *who bars the door with outstretched arms*.)

PATRICIA

Michael!

WALLY

What's going on here?

CLEOTA

(*Peering at fight off-scene*)

Godamighty!

PATRICIA

Oh—Michael, stop them! Wally, stop them!

MICHAEL

No, don't stop them! Let Mr. Turner alone and he'll tear him to pieces!

(*Crash outside.*)

WALLY

Get away from that door! (*He hurls* MICHAEL *aside.* PATRICIA *runs and kneels beside* MICHAEL.)

PATRICIA

Michael! Michael!

(ELLEN *re-enters the front door, calling:*)

ELLEN

Joe, are you coming? (*She sees* MICHAEL *and* PATRICIA *on the floor, and looks around the room for* TOMMY *and* JOE. MICHAEL *continues to quote poetry dramatically.*)

MICHAEL

(*With rapid fervor*)

"And many-a-broken heart is here . . ."

ELLEN

What is it?

MICHAEL

"And many-a-broken head,
But tomorrow—by the living God!—
We'll try the game again!"
(*He tries to rise;* PATRICIA *drops him in disgust.*)

PATRICIA

Oh, Michael!
(JOE *and* WALLY *carry in the unconscious* TOMMY, *and deposit him on the sofa.*)

ELLEN

(*Screams*)

Tommy!!
(*The phone rings insistently.*)

CLEOTA

(*Shouts imperturbably into phone*)
Professah Turner's res-i-dence!

The Curtain Falls Swiftly

ACT THREE

ACT THREE

SCENE: *The Turner living room. Same as Acts One and Two.*

About noon, Monday.

The room is neat and orderly, but the flowers and other signs of festivity have been removed.

The stage is empty, but the telephone bell is ringing. A moment later, the doorbell also begins to sound insistently. CLEOTA *enters from the dining room, wiping her hands on her apron, scuttles for an instant between the bells, picks up phone.*

CLEOTA
(*Into phone*)

Stop ringin' dis thing both at once . . . Who? . . . Ah cain' heah you foh de ringin'. Hol' on . . . (*Putting down the receiver, she hurries to the front door and opens it cautiously, bracing herself to prevent a forced entrance. She speaks through the crack of the door to the man standing there*) Ah tol' you stop ringin' eve'ything. Ah'm heah, ain' I?

REPORTER

I'd like to see Mr. Turner.

CLEOTA

Is you a newspapah?

REPORTER

Yeh, I'm from the *Daily Journal*.

CLEOTA

He cain' see nobody—he's sick.

REPORTER

I know—but will he be up today? Is he going to his class?

CLEOTA

He ain' goin' nowheah. His haid huhts him. He's sick. Go 'way. (*She forces the door shut, returns to the telephone*) Professah Turner's res-i-dence. . . . *Daily* what? . . . You jus' *was* heah. . . . No, Professah Turner ain' talkin' to nobody. He's sick in bed with his haid. . . . No, he ain' goin' an' you ain' comin'. He ain' not talkin' 'cause he doan wanta talk. He jus' ain' talkin' cause he cain' talk. Goo'bye. (*The bolted door is rattled from outside, then the doorbell begins to ring insistently.* CLEOTA *looks at the door angrily and starts for it. She looks back at the phone and mutters*) What's goin' on heah? . . . I told you to go 'way. (*She opens the door and* PATRICIA *enters.*)

PATRICIA

What's the matter?

CLEOTA

(*Giggling in embarrassment*)

Oh, it's you. I thought it was that newspapah again. He jus' went.

PATRICIA

He didn't go—he's outside picketing. Where's my sister, Cleota?

CLEOTA

Upstaihs . . . Miss Patricia, Ah wish Ah knew bettah what's goin' on heah.

PATRICIA

Never mind.

CLEOTA

Mr. Michael jus' left.

PATRICIA

Oh. Well, if Mr. Michael Barnes comes here again, *don't let him in!*

CLEOTA

No, ma'am. (CLEOTA *goes into the dining room just as* ELLEN, *looking very depressed, comes from upstairs.*)

PATRICIA

Hello, Ellen. How's Tommy? Is he still asleep?

ELLEN

Yes, but he tosses around and mutters. The doctor says he can get up this afternoon.

PATRICIA

No concussion, then?

ELLEN

Yes, a little.

147

PATRICIA

(Seating herself on settee)

I guess when anybody's as crazy as Tommy or Michael, a little concussion doesn't make any difference.

ELLEN

Did you get the butter?

PATRICIA

Oh, Lord, no. I'll go back.

ELLEN

Never mind. I need a little air. (PATRICIA *tackles the problem in the air with the light attitude of youth, becoming serious as she realizes more vigorous methods are needed.*)

PATRICIA

How's *your* head?

ELLEN

Oh, all right.

PATRICIA

Is it? Say, what is this second springtime you're all going through, anyway?

ELLEN

Tommy won't let me in on what he's really thinking about. He thinks I'm not smart enough to understand it—that's what it comes down to.

PATRICIA

Oh, a mental problem. I haven't been exactly listening at

148

keyholes, but isn't there a Joe Something-or-other mixed up in this?

ELLEN

Oh, there's more to it than a fight about Joe.

PATRICIA

Pretty good one round here Saturday about Joe. (*Then, directly*) You know Tommy was fighting for you in his mid-Victorian way, don't you?

ELLEN

Oh, but he was drunk. When he's sober he despises me. He thinks I'm a dim-wit.

PATRICIA

Oh, he wouldn't want you any other way than you are.

ELLEN

Thanks.

PATRICIA

I mean you're smart enough for Tommy, and you know it, and he knows it.

ELLEN
(*Unhappily*)

I'm all mixed up. I want to go away some place where I can think.

PATRICIA

Look: this is a new century. You're not Diana-of-the-Crossways or somebody.

149

ELLEN

Well, what do you want me to do—stay here when he doesn't want me?

PATRICIA

(*Vigorously*)

No, but if you're going away, go away with Joe. Tommy's certainly been throwing you at him. Why don't you take him up on it? See what happens.

ELLEN

Is this advice to the lovelorn? Do you think he would come running after me?

PATRICIA

Well, you've got to quit moping around and do something. I thought we Stanley women were supposed to have some resources. (*Rises and faces* ELLEN) Look, your great-grandmother chased her man all the way to Nebraska in a covered wagon.

ELLEN

Well, I'm not going to chase anybody anywhere! I'm going to talk this over with Tommy, fairly and squarely, face to face. (*Starts to front door.*)

PATRICIA

"Fairly and squarely!" How did your generation ever get through the 1920's?

ELLEN

(*Sadly*)

We didn't. (*She goes out.*)

(PATRICIA *sighs in despair.* TOMMY *comes slowly down-*

stairs. He wears a terry-cloth bathrobe, and has a wet turkish towel twisted about his head.)

TOMMY

Hello, Pat.

PATRICIA

Tommy—you shouldn't be up!

TOMMY

I'm all right. What day is this?

PATRICIA

Monday.

TOMMY

Cleota! Cleota! (*To* PATRICIA) Can I take this thing off?

PATRICIA

You're not supposed to. You ought to lie down. (TOMMY *sinks in chair.*)

TOMMY

I'll just lean back. (*Winces as he tries it*) No—I guess I won't.

(CLEOTA *appears in dining-room door.*)

CLEOTA

Mistah Turner—is you up?

TOMMY

Yes, I'm up. Cleota, don't let anyone in this house except Mr. Michael Barnes.

(PATRICIA *shakes her head "No" to* CLEOTA.)

CLEOTA

(*Nodding to both*)

Yessuh—Ah do de best Ah can. (*Backs out of room.*)

TOMMY

Where's Ellen?

PATRICIA

She went out to—to get the transfer man—for her trunk.

TOMMY

She's going away?

PATRICIA

Oh, no. She just likes to call on transfer men. Didn't you know that?

TOMMY

I can't stand irony so early in the day, Patricia.

PATRICIA

You're all right now, you see. She wouldn't go before. I don't know why.

TOMMY

You ought to know why. Your sister wouldn't walk out on anybody when he's down—even when he's down with delirium tremens.

PATRICIA

You didn't have D.T.'s. You had concussion.

152

TOMMY

Seemed more like D.T.'s.

PATRICIA

You don't know very much about my little sister, do you?

TOMMY

I know a lot more than I did last Friday. I think I will lie down. (*Goes to sofa.*)

PATRICIA

Why do you have to make everything as hard as you can? (TOMMY *groans a little with pain*) Do you want another cold towel?

TOMMY

No, thanks.
   (*Phone rings.*)

PATRICIA
   (*Answering phone*)
Yes? . . . Who? No, Michael Barnes isn't here.

TOMMY
   (*Lying down carefully*)
He was here and he's coming back.

PATRICIA

This is Patricia Stanley. . . . Yes . . . Yes . . . I'll be very glad to tell him to call you—if I see him. Good-bye. (*Slams receiver down*) That was Hot Garters Gardner!

TOMMY

Oh. Why did she call here?

PATRICIA

She said they told her Michael was on his way here, but obviously she just called for my benefit . . . So that's where

he went Saturday night! You had that Hot—that Miss Gardner in some of your classes; do you remember her?

TOMMY

(*Reflectively*)

I don't know. What does she look like?

PATRICIA

Well, she—doesn't wear any . . . (*Gestures a brassière.*)

TOMMY

I only had her in Wordsworth.

PATRICIA

Calling up here! (*There is a knock at the door;* PATRICIA *smiles grimly. She goes to the door and opens it.* MICHAEL *steps in; he is taken aback at seeing* PATRICIA) Good morning, Michael. Come in.

TOMMY
(*In warning, sepulchral tones*)
Yes, come in, Michael. (PATRICIA's *back is turned so* TOMMY *pantomimes "telephone" for* MICHAEL's *benefit.* MICHAEL *peers at him nervously.*)

MICHAEL

I got the car for you. . . . Feel better now that you're up? (*Doesn't get the pantomime.*)

TOMMY

Yes, much better. How do you feel?

MICHAEL

I feel all right.

TOMMY

That's good. (*Mimics* PATRICIA's *brassière gesture.*)

PATRICIA
(*Turning*)
If you'll excuse me . . .

155

MICHAEL

Oh, Pat, wait! I—could I talk to you for a minute? Couldn't we go outside there and . . .

PATRICIA

No, we couldn't go outside there! Is it anything you're ashamed to say in front of Tommy?

MICHAEL
(Stiffening)

No. No, I'm not. Only— Well, I don't want to get off on the wrong foot again. I'm sorry I got so mad Saturday. I said things and did things that . . .

PATRICIA

You certainly did!

MICHAEL

Well, I'm sorry, and . . . Oh, Pat, you ought to be able to see this my way. We just lost our tempers and—well—Mr. Turner and I are in a jam. I think you ought to—well—make an effort to understand what we're trying to do and stand by us—that is, if you care anything about me at all.

PATRICIA
(So sweetly)

Oh, I certainly do. I've been standing by—taking messages for you—phone calls. I'm so glad we had this nice talk. *(Shakes his hand)* And before you go, be sure to call Maple 4307! *(She hurls the last at him furiously, then sweeps out the front door.)*

MICHAEL

(*Looking after her*)

Maple 430 . . . (*Horrified, as he realizes who the number belongs to*) Did The Garters call here?

TOMMY

That's what I was trying to tell you. Patricia answered the phone. The—elastics—snapped right in her face.

MICHAEL

And I didn't even *do* anything. (*Sits beside* TOMMY *on sofa*) I hope.

TOMMY

Michael, you're making me nervous.
(*A pause.*)

MICHAEL

Will you be able to go to the faculty meeting tonight?

TOMMY

I'll be there.

MICHAEL

They'll be out to get you. . . . I know this is all my fault, Mr. Turner.

TOMMY

Yes, you're certainly the man that lighted the match.

MICHAEL

I just came from the president's office; he flayed me alive.

TOMMY

Are you kicked out?

MICHAEL

Suspended.

TOMMY

Michael, tell me . . . are you really a Communist?

MICHAEL

Me? No. I only know one guy who is. I'm—well, I guess I'm an unconfused liberal. . . . I think I'll go to Stringfellow Barr's School in Annapolis and read the classics.

TOMMY

I wonder where I'll go?
> (ELLEN *enters front door with parcel.*)

MICHAEL
(Rises)

Hello, Mrs. Turner.

ELLEN

Good morning. (*Sees* TOMMY) Good morning, Tommy. . . . (*Goes to dining-room door and calls*) Cleota . . .

TOMMY

Good morning.
> (CLEOTA *enters.*)

ELLEN

Here's the butter, Cleota. Will you make Mr. Turner a cup of tea? (*Turns back to him*) Would you like a hard-boiled egg?

158

TOMMY

No, thanks. Nothing hard. My teeth hurt.
(CLEOTA *retires*.)

ELLEN

Are you waiting for Patricia, Michael?

MICHAEL

I saw her. I'm leaving town, Mrs. Turner.

ELLEN

I'm awfully sorry, Michael.

WALLY
(*Off-stage*)

Pat! Oh, Pat!

ELLEN

Come in, Wally. (WALLY *comes in from the garden*) Patricia's gone out somewhere.

WALLY

Oh, I see. (*To* MICHAEL) You waiting for her?

MICHAEL

That's none of your business. Why? (*He strides over to* WALLY.)

WALLY
(*Lowers his voice*)

I know what you did Saturday night, that's why. Well,

thanks, Mrs. Turner. I just cut across the back way. I'll walk on down to the house. (*Starts out.*)

MICHAEL
(*Stops him*)
I think I'll walk along down to the house. I want to talk to you.

WALLY
You don't have to.

MICHAEL
If I didn't have to, I wouldn't do it. I'm no masochist. (*Starts out.* WALLY *stares after him blankly, then follows.*)

WALLY
You don't have to use words like that in front of ladies!

MICHAEL
I'll be back in time to drive you to class, Mr. Turner.
(*Both boys go out.*)

TOMMY
Thanks.
(CLEOTA *enters, and* ELLEN *takes the tray from her.*)

ELLEN
Here's your tea.
(CLEOTA *goes out.*)

TOMMY
Thanks.

160

ELLEN

(*With some constraint*)

How do you feel?

TOMMY

Very strange.

ELLEN

Is everything clear to you now?

TOMMY

Clear in the center. It's kind of fuzzy around the edges.
(ELLEN *has made up her mind what she wants to say;
she seats herself and begins.*)

ELLEN

I hope it's clear enough to give me a chance to say something, without your going off on one of your literary tangents.

TOMMY

I don't do that.

ELLEN

I know you think I'm not very bright or something
(TOMMY *tries to demur, but she continues*) but you must
realize that you got me all mixed up Friday, and that you
were even less helpful Saturday.

TOMMY

That wasn't me Saturday. That was a drunken sea-lion.

ELLEN

I rather liked you as a sea-lion.

TOMMY

Yes, I must have been very funny. Did you ever read Hodgson's poem, "The Bull"?

ELLEN

Oh, Tommy!

TOMMY

It's the story of the defeated male. There is no defeat that can be quite so complete.

ELLEN

You wouldn't admit that this defeat was on account of —— No, it has to be something out of a book.

TOMMY

"When the bull's head is in the dust, life goes on and leaves him there"; it's a psychological fact. The poets understand these things.

ELLEN

And all the cows react the same way? As if they were reading instructions from a blackboard? Oh, Tommy, listen to me . . .

(*The doorbell rings.*)

TOMMY

The point is, I don't want any pity.

CLEOTA

(*Hurrying from dining room*)

It's dat prize-fightah! I seen him from de windah!

162

(ELLEN *admits* JOE, *who comes in without his old bounce; he is worried and restless.*)

ELLEN

Hello, Joe.

JOE

Hello. Hello. (*Awkwardly, to* TOMMY.)

TOMMY

Hello.

JOE

I'm sorry, Tommy. I didn't hit you hard. You slipped and hit your head on a bench.

TOMMY

Yeh, I know. What's the matter with your hand?

JOE

You kinda bit me. . . . Ed's out in the car. We just chased a reporter away hanging around out there.

ELLEN

Well, don't let any reporters in, Cleota.

TOMMY

And don't let Keller in.
    (CLEOTA *nods and exits to kitchen.*)

JOE
    (*Indicating wet towel*)
Do you have to keep that thing on?

163

TOMMY

No, I just do it because I like it. (*Throws down towel.*)

JOE

Could I have a little slug of something? I . . .

ELLEN

Certainly. Scotch?

JOE

Yeh, fine. (ELLEN *goes to dining room.* JOE *paces*) I got the galloping jumps. I can use a little drink. Haven't slept for two nights.

TOMMY

Worrying about something?

JOE

Yeh, worrying about something. And my cold's worse.

TOMMY

Want some Kleenex?

JOE

(*Irritated*)

No, I don't want some Kleenex! Damn reporters been bothering me, too.

TOMMY

What do they want with you?

JOE

Oh, they wanted me to pick an All-American team.

164

TOMMY

(*Incredulously—almost*)

Did you?

JOE

Yeh. Kinda took my mind off things.

TOMMY

(*Sarcastically*)

Who'd you pick for right guard?

JOE

Shulig—Kansas State Teachers'. (*Faces* TOMMY) Look, Tommy, where the hell do we all stand now? (TOMMY *picks up towel, presses it to his head again*) Does that kinda throb?

TOMMY

No.

JOE

Well, I wanta know where we all stand.

TOMMY

Oh, let it alone, Joe. It'll work out. You and I can handle this. I don't want Ellen worried about details now. She's got enough trouble with me—sitting around the house looking like a hot-oil shampoo. . . .

(ELLEN *enters with bowl of ice. She fixes a drink.*)

ELLEN

There's been more drinking in this house in the last two days than we've done in ten years.

(JOE *sits on settee at far side of room.*)

165

TOMMY

(*After a pause*)

Ellen, Joe picked Shulig of Kansas State Teachers' for right guard, on his All-American. Isn't that nice?

(ELLEN *looks annoyed.*)

JOE

(*Reminiscently*)

It was kinda hard choosing between him and Feldkamp of Western Reserve. Both big and fast.

ELLEN

(*Crossing with drink*)

Here you are, dear. (*She is coolly oblivious of* TOMMY's *hand which he puts out for the drink; goes on to* JOE, *who doesn't realize she means him*) Dear. (*He looks up at her with a start, glances at* TOMMY, *then takes the drink.*)

TOMMY

(*Sulkily*)

I don't want any.

JOE

Say, have you got a Pennsylvania timetable around?

ELLEN

Where are you going, Joe?

JOE

Well, I've got to be in Washington tomorrow.

ELLEN

That's going to rush me.

JOE

What do you mean?

ELLEN

Well, Joe, I thought you and I might start out by going up to that little inn at Granville tonight. Just for a few days. (*She sits close to* JOE *on settee.*)

TOMMY
(*Rises*)

What did you say?

ELLEN
(*To* JOE)

I think it's the nicest place around here. Don't you?

JOE
(*Flopping on the hook*)

I—I—eh— Could I have a little more Scotch? (*He hurries across the room, pours himself another drink.*)

ELLEN
(*Gaily*)

I don't want you to get drunk, Joe.

JOE

I'll be all right—I'll be all right. What time is it?

167

TOMMY

Never mind what time it is. (*To* ELLEN) Would you mind explaining this a little better?

ELLEN

I'll try to make it as clear as I can for both of you. I simply have to make a fresh start now, Tommy. You understand women; you must see that. I can't stay here now. You've made your plans, and now I have to make mine.

TOMMY

Yes—but not like this—not running off to Granville!

ELLEN

All right, if you're afraid of a scandal, we'll go farther away. Put Granville out of your mind, then. We'll go directly to Pittsburgh.

JOE

Huh?

ELLEN

It's a very big town. Nobody need know anything about it.

JOE

About what?

ELLEN

About us. About our living together.
(*Both men stop cold.*)

TOMMY

Ellen!

168

JOE

(*Desperately*)

But you see—I don't live in Pittsburgh. (*He makes a large circular gesture with both hands*) I live in Sewickly. (*The*

gesture is small and loving now) And my boss lives there, too. And my mother. My mother's not very well. My mother . . .

TOMMY

Oh, you and your mother!

JOE

Besides it's a Presbyterian town.

169

ELLEN

You're not being very gallant, Joe.

TOMMY

No. Are you trying to get out of this?

JOE

No, but I come from a long line of married people! And besides, I'm not going to Pittsburgh directly. I've got to go to Washington, and that's one place I couldn't take you, Ellen!

TOMMY

You'll take her any place she wants to go, but she's not going any place!

ELLEN

Oh, yes, I am!
    (*There is a loud knock, and* ED KELLER *enters.*)

ED

I can't sit out in that car all day, you know.

JOE

Oh, I'm sorry, Ed, but—jees, I forgot all about you. (*Turns to* TOMMY) I persuaded Ed to come over and talk to you before this thing gets too bad. (*He leads* ED *over to* TOMMY.)

TOMMY

It couldn't get any worse!

JOE

I mean about the trustees.

170

TOMMY

Let the trustees take care of themselves. We have troubles of our own.

ED

You'll find out this is your trouble. Is he able to talk?

JOE

God, yes!

ED

(*To* TOMMY)

Well, then, listen. We just had a trustees' meeting in the president's office. Michael Barnes is out, and you're on your way out. You'll be asked to resign tonight.

ELLEN

(*Rises*)

Oh, Tommy!

JOE

Ed's trying to help him while there's still time. After to-night, it will be too late.

TOMMY

What do you care what happens tonight? You'll be in Granville or somewhere.

ED

What're you going to be doing in Granville?

TOMMY

Please don't ask personal questions!

ELLEN

Do you mind if I stay a little while, Tommy?

TOMMY

(*Angrily*)

Why shouldn't you stay? It's your house.

ED

Sit down, Ellen. (*She sits. To* TOMMY) There's just one thing you can do: come out with a statement to the papers, quick. Say you were sick. Say you didn't know anything about Barnes' editorial. You think it's an outrage. You're not going to read this Vanzetti thing, and you think Barnes is getting what he deserves. That's the only thing that'll save your neck.

ELLEN

Tommy wouldn't say that about Michael, Ed, and you shouldn't ask him to.

TOMMY

Thank you!

ED

All right, then. That's all I had to say. Good-bye. This is on your own head.

ELLEN

Ed. Just a minute, please. (*Faces* TOMMY) I know that reading this letter must mean something to you, Tommy. Something none of us can quite understand. I wish I could. It might help me to understand a lot of other things, when I can get away where I can think.

TOMMY

Such as what?

172

ELLEN

Such as what is important to you. What you've been fighting for. Whether it's something you really believe in and love, or just your own selfish pride. I think you got into this just because you were mad at me. And that's ridiculous, because now you don't care what I do or say about it. You're out of that.

ED

(*To* JOE)

I don't see what she's talking about. (JOE *motions him to be quiet.*)

TOMMY

All right, I'll try to explain what it means to me. Perhaps, originally, pride had something to do with this. And jealousy.

ELLEN

And stubbornness. . . .

TOMMY

And—please. I am trying to say that—now—I am not fighting about you and me at all. This is bigger than you and me or any of us.

ELLEN

Is it?

ED

(*Ironically*)

It must be a masterpiece. That letter must be quite a nice piece of propaganda.

TOMMY

Why don't you read it and find out?

173

ED
I don't read things like that.

TOMMY
My God, you don't even know what you're objecting to!

JOE
Well, Tommy, why don't you read the letter to us, and let us see what it is?

TOMMY
I'll be glad to read it to you, but I'll read it to my class, too. (*He goes to bookcase and hunts for the book; not finding it, he remembers it is upstairs and goes up.*)

ED
You don't have to read it to me. I know what kind of stuff it is.

> (*The front door bursts open, and* PATRICIA *backs in, followed by* WALLY, *leaving the door open.*)

PATRICIA
But I can't go with you now! I told you I've got to wait here and see what Tommy's going to do.

WALLY
But you're not going to the class! You said you're not going!

PATRICIA
I'm not! I just want to know!

174

WALLY

I'll bet you *are* going! You're waiting here for Michael to go with you!

PATRICIA

Oh, go away! (*Turning, she sees the others, who are listening*) Oh—I'm sorry. (*She rushes across to the door leading to the garden.*)

ED

What's this now?

JOE

(*Grinning*)

Hey, Pat, you better think twice before you scrap with Wally here. He's coming in with me at Pittsburgh next year.

WALLY

A lot she cares about Pittsburgh! I run sixty-two yards through Michigan, and all she wants is to listen to Mike Barnes talk about free love. (*He stalks over to* PATRICIA.)

ED

She does?

ELLEN

(*Trying to stop* WALLY)

Uh—Wally, how's Stalenkiwiecz?

WALLY

(*Brushing past her*)

He's much better. (*To* PATRICIA) If you knew what I know about that guy Barnes . . .

175

PATRICIA

I know what you're hinting at! And what if he did? It only shows what an intense person Michael is! I know that no matter what he did, he was thinking of me!

WALLY

That's disgusting!

PATRICIA

And aren't you a little bit disgusting to mention it? I thought *men* had some loyalty! (*She goes out.*)

WALLY

(*Following her out*)

Now, listen here . . . I want to tell you about that guy. Do you know what he did? . . .

ED

(*Sitting on sofa*)

What kind of a house is this?

(*As* TOMMY *comes downstairs with an open book in his hand,* DAMON, *carrying his ever-present umbrella, walks quietly in the open front door and looks around.*)

TOMMY

All right, here it is. Now sit down—or stand up—but listen! Oh, hello, Dr. Damon. You're just in time.

DAMON

In time for what? (*Sees* ED, *moves toward him*) Oh, has the Inquisition moved its headquarters?

176

TOMMY

I'm just going to read the Inquisition a letter from one of its victims.

ED

That's about enough of that.

DAMON

Gentlemen, gentlemen. This may not be wise, Thomas.

TOMMY

It may not be wise, but it's necessary. I think you'll have to take a stand, too, Dr. Damon.

DAMON

I hope not. (*Sits on settee;* JOE *seats himself on the fireplace bench;* ELLEN *sits at opposite side of room.*)

TOMMY

So did I hope not. I didn't start out to lead a crusade. I simply mentioned one day that I meant to read to my class three letters by men whose profession was not literature, but who had something sincere to say. Once I had declared that very harmless intention, the world began to shake, great institutions trembled, and football players descended upon me and my wife! I realized then that I was doing something important.

ED
(*Sarcastically*)

You make it sound mighty innocent. Reading Lincoln and General Sherman—and Vanzetti. What was the reason you gave for picking out Vanzetti?

177

TOMMY

(*To* ED)

Originally I chose him to show that what we call broken English can sometimes be very moving and eloquent, but now—

ED

We wouldn't object if this was just a case of broken English—it's more than that.

TOMMY

Yes, you've made it more than that.

ED

Vanzetti was an anarchist! He was executed for murder.

TOMMY

He was accused of murder, but thousands of people believe he was executed simply because of the ideas he believed in.

ED

That's a dangerous thing to bring up.

TOMMY

(*Getting really mad*)

No, it's a dangerous thing to keep down. I'm fighting for a teacher's rights, but if you want to make it political, all right! You can't suppress ideas because you don't like them— not in this country—not yet. This is a university! (*To* DAMON) It's our business to bring what light we can into this muddled world—to try to follow truth!

DAMON

You are quite right, Thomas, but I wish you would make an effort not to—uh—uh—intone.

TOMMY

I'm not intoning—I'm yelling! And for God's sake, sir, put away that umbrella! (DAMON *covers his umbrella with his hat*) Don't you see: this isn't about Vanzetti; this is about us! If I can't read this letter today, tomorrow none of us will be able to teach anything except what Mr. Keller here and the legislature permit us to teach. Can't you see what that leads to—what it has led to in other places? We're holding the last fortress of free thought, and if we surrender to prejudice and dictation, we're cowards! (*He strides across the room.*)

ELLEN

Tommy, no matter how deeply you feel about this, what can you *do*? What can any one man do? Except to lose everything . . .

TOMMY

Ellen, I have very little more to lose. And I can't tell you what I hope to gain. I can't answer that. I only know that I have to do it.

(PATRICIA *appears in the doorway, stops and listens.*)

DAMON

May we hear the letter—in a slightly calmer mood, perhaps?

TOMMY

Yes, sir . . . This may disappoint you a little, Mr. Keller.

It isn't inflammatory, so it may make you feel a little silly. At least, I hope so. . . . (*He holds up the book, pauses.* ED *and* JOE *get set in their chairs*) Vanzetti wrote this in April, 1927, after he was sentenced to die. It has been printed in many newspapers. It appears in this book. You could destroy every printed copy of it, but it would not die out of the language, because a great many people know it by heart. (*He reads, hardly referring to the book, watching them*) "If it had not been for these thing, I might have live out my life talking at street corners to scorning men. I might have die, unmarked, unknown, a failure. Now we are not a failure. Never in our full life could we hope to do so much work for tolerance, for Justice, for man's understanding of man, as now we do by accident. Our words—our lives—our pain—nothing! The taking of our lives—the lives of a good shoe-maker and a poor fish-peddler—all! That last moment belongs to us —that agony is our triumph!" . . . Well, that's it! (*He closes the book and drops it on the table. There is silence for a moment;* KELLER *is puzzled;* ELLEN, *who has been moved by the letter, looks up in surprise, meets* TOMMY's *eyes, then drops hers.*)

JOE
(*Uncomfortably*)
Well, that isn't so bad! That isn't a bad letter.

ED
Is that all of it?

TOMMY
Yes, that's all!

180

JOE
(*Rises*)

Maybe Tommy's right. I don't see that it would do so much harm.

ED
(*Slowly*)

Yes, it will. If he reads this letter to his class he'll get a lot of those kids worried about that man. Make socialists out of 'em.

JOE

It's got me worried already.

ED
(*Rises, facing* TOMMY)

No—I won't have it. You fellows are trying to defy the authority of the trustees. You say you're going to take a stand. Well, we've *taken* a stand. I wouldn't care if that letter were by Alexander Hamilton.

TOMMY
(*Measuring him*)

Neither would I! The principle is exactly the same.

JOE
(*Speaking hopefully*)

Well, then, read something else. Why can't you read Hoover?

181

ED

Yeah.

JOE

He writes a lot of stuff—a lot of good stuff in his book.

TOMMY

(*His artistic ire is aroused*)

Hoover can't *write* as well as Vanzetti.

ED

(*Winces*)

That's a terrible thing to say. You'll get in trouble saying things like that.

TOMMY

Very likely! (*He strides to garden door.*)

JOE

Ed, look—can't we compromise somehow? Seems a shame that a little thing like this should . . .

ELLEN

(*Rises*)

It isn't little! Joe, you have some influence around here.

TOMMY

I can fight my own battles, Ellen.

ELLEN

Can't I say anything any more—even on your side?

182

ED

Turner, I've heard the letter and . . .

TOMMY

(*Answering* ELLEN)

Not out of a sense of self-sacrifice or something!

ED

What?

ELLEN

Oh, yes, you always know . . .

ED

(*To* JOE)

Do we always have to have women butting into this?

JOE

Ellen isn't women. She's Tommy's wife.

ELLEN

(*Furiously*)

No, I'm not!

ED

No. Turner, it comes to this. . . . (*Turns to* ELLEN) You're not what? Do you mean to stand there and tell me you two are not—

TOMMY

(*Raging*)

Will you please not ask personal questions?

183

ED

(*To* TOMMY)

No. *We can't have that in this school!*

ELLEN

(*With a glance at* JOE)

It's Joe and I who are going to live together!

ED

Yeh, will you let me— (*To* ELLEN) You and Joe are going to what! (*Turns on* JOE) What the hell is going on here anyway?

JOE

Now don't look at me!

ED

You can't live with Ellen!

JOE

I didn't say . . .

ELLEN

(*Twisting the knife in both men's backs*)

We might as well tell him now. I'm going to Pittsburgh with Joe. (*Plants herself on settee.*)

ED

(*Turning back to* ELLEN)

Why, you can't do that! The newspapers would make Mid-western University look like some kind of a honky-tonk or something! Why, this is worse than that goddamn letter!

184

TOMMY

Aren't you getting off the subject?

ED

No! What kind of a woman are you?

TOMMY

(*Advancing on* ED)

Why don't you come out in the back yard?

JOE

Better be careful, Ed!

ELLEN

No more fights, please!

DAMON

(*Rises*)

I think I shall get a breath of fresh air. (*Goes to front door and opens it.*)

ELLEN

Well, I can't stay *here* now!

JOE

Look, Ed, you don't understand. You get things all mixed up.

ED

Well, I've got this much straight—if we can keep sex out of this for a minute! I came here to say to you that if you read this letter today you're out of this university tomorrow! You take this stand and you stand alone!

185

DAMON

(Turning, walks deliberately over to ED)

Mr. Keller, for forty-two years I have followed a policy of appeasement. I might say I have been kicked around in this institution by one Edward K. Keller after another. . . .

ED

There is only one Edward K. Keller.

DAMON

There has always been at least one. But there is an increasing element in the faculty which resents your attitude toward any teacher who raises his voice or so much as clears his throat. I warn you that if you persist in persecuting Thomas Turner, you will have a fight on your hands, my friend.

ED

Do you think that Bryson and Kressinger and I are afraid of a few dissatisfied book-worms who work for twenty-five hundred dollars a year?

DAMON

(With strong indignation)

These men are not malcontents! Some of them are distinguished scholars who have made this university what it is!

ED

(Aghast)

They've made it what it is! What about me? Who's getting this new stadium? Who brought Coach Sprague here from Southern Methodist?

186

JOE

He means that this thing is bigger than stadiums and coaches, Ed.

ED

Nothing's bigger than the new stadium.

JOE

We've all had a bad week-end around here, Ed, and you're not helping any.

ED

Do you think I've had a good week-end!
(MICHAEL *and* NUTSY *come in the front door.*)

MICHAEL

Come in, Nutsy.

ED

Now what!?

MICHAEL

We're circulating petitions for Mr. Turner. Show 'em, Nutsy.

NUTSY

(*Whipping out some sheets full of signatures*)
This one's just from 14th Avenue and the Athletic House. We've got 357 names.

DAMON

We want no student insurrections!

JOE

Let me see that thing. (*Takes petition from* NUTSY, *scans it hurriedly.*)

187

ED

You're wasting your time with that handful of names. Turner will be out tomorrow and Barnes is on his way home now.

MICHAEL

I'm not on my way home yet, sir.

ED

Oɦɦɦ! So you're Barnes!!! So you're the little puppy that called me a Fascist!

(PATRICIA *comes between* ED *and* MICHAEL.)

PATRICIA
(*To* ED)

Well, the way you're treating everybody, I think you are a Fascist!

ELLEN

Patricia!

TOMMY

Let her alone!

ELLEN

Oh, she can stand up for Michael, but I can't stand up for you! Is that it?

TOMMY

It's not the same.

ED

Do I have to stand here and be insulted by every sixteen-year-old child that comes into this room?

PATRICIA

I'm not sixteen, I'm nineteen!

188

MICHAEL

She'll soon be twenty!

ED

Why don't *you* get packing?

MICHAEL

You don't need to worry about me. I'll be far away from here by tomorrow. Come on, Nutsy! (NUTSY *starts out,* MICHAEL *following.*)

PATRICIA

If you throw him out, I'm going with him! Wait, Michael! (*Starts after him.*)

ED

Are you married to that little radical?

PATRICIA

You don't have to be married to somebody to go away with him—*do you, Ellen?* (*She and* MICHAEL *go out.*)

DAMON

(*Who can't cope with any more*)
I think I shall go home, have my Ovaltine and lie down. (*He goes out the front door.*)

ED

He'll need his Ovaltine.

JOE

(*Suddenly, awesomely*)
Say, Ed, look. This thing has been signed by Stalenkiwiecz and Wierasocka.

ED

What! I don't believe it! (*Snatches petition, scans it, in all its terrible significance.*)

JOE

Ed, you ought to have some respect for men like Dean Damon and Stalenkiwiecz and Wierasocka.

ED

(*Stricken*)

They can't do this to me! Two of the biggest men in the university signing the red petition! You, the greatest half-back we ever had, running away with a woman! Why— *they'll never ask us to the Rose Bowl now!*

TOMMY

What is the Rose Bowl?
 (ED *almost screams.*)

ED

I'm getting out of this house! Coming, Joe?

JOE

No.

ED

By God, you can't depend on anybody! I've a damn good notion to resign from the board of trustees. (*Stiffening*) But I'll kick you out if it's the last thing I do.

TOMMY

(*Grimly*)

Just to make things even—I'll kick you out. Here's your hat. (*Gives him* JOE's *derby.*)

ED

Very well! (*Puts on hat and leaves angrily.*)

JOE

Hey, that's *my* hat!

TOMMY

Well, get another one! (*He closes door.*) Well, that's that. (*They look at each other. Here they are again; the triangle.*)

JOE

Yeh, that's that. (*Pause. He eyes the others doubtfully*) Well, I s'pose Ed will never speak to me again.

TOMMY

I have to go to class. I'll be late. (*Starts for stairs.*)

ELLEN

(*Appealingly, to* TOMMY)

Tommy, I . . .

TOMMY

I know. I know.

ELLEN

You know what?

TOMMY

I know what you're going to say—but I don't want substitutes. I don't want *loyalty.*

(ELLEN *turns away.*)

JOE

What's the matter with that?

TOMMY

I just don't want Ellen standing by like a Red Cross nurse because she knows I'm in trouble!

JOE

I don't know whether you need a nurse or a psychoanalyst!

ELLEN

I think he's analyzed it very well himself. It isn't because you think I don't care, it's because you don't.

TOMMY

(*Almost bursting*)
I thought we could settle this *quietly* and *calmly*.

ELLEN

Quietly and calmly! Oh, God! (*She picks up large ash tray from a table and smashes it on the floor.*)

TOMMY

Now, don't do that! I can throw things, too! (*He picks up his tea-cup.*)

ELLEN

No, you can't—you haven't got enough blood in you! (TOMMY *glares at her, puts cup down coldly, suddenly snatches it up, and hurls it into the fireplace, reaches for the saucer.*)

JOE

(*Leaps for* TOMMY, *grabs the saucer from him*)
Now wait—let me handle this. *I don't throw things.* . . . I

192

just want to say that I came to this city *to see a football game. . . .*

ELLEN

(*Right into* JOE's *face*)

Oh, no, you didn't! You came for me. You haven't been ere for a ball game in ten years. You wait till Brenda and you are separated, then you come for me!

JOE

Oh, hell! (*Throws the saucer in fireplace, then wilts as he realizes this household has affected him, too.*)

TOMMY

(*Desperately insisting upon his doom*)

That's very smart, Ellen. That's very penetrating. That's all I wanted to know. (*To* JOE) Subconsciously, you came here for Ellen, so don't try to deny it.

JOE

I don't do things subconsciously! You're full of childish explanations of every goddamn thing that comes up!

TOMMY

And you're full of psychological evasions!

ELLEN

(*Screaming. It's a mad-house now*)

Oh, shut up! I am not going to listen to any more of this! (*She runs upstairs.* TOMMY *sits limply on sofa and covers his face with his hands. There is a long pause.*)

JOE

(*Slowly, and with determination*)

Well, I'll tell you one thing! I'm not going upstairs this time! If you'd explained what you were standing for on Saturday, things would have cleared up around here and I'd be in Washington now, talking to Ickes.

194

TOMMY

(*In a low grim tone*)

Are you still in love with Norma?

JOE

Norma who?

TOMMY

Your wife.

JOE

My wife's name is Brenda. And you're not going to talk her over with me. I can't be alone with you two minutes and have any private life left!

ELLEN

(*From upstairs*)

Tommy! *What did you do with my nail file??!*

JOE

Oh, God—she sounds worse than last Saturday!

TOMMY

I haven't got it. (*He absently goes through a pocket, finds it, brings it out*) Oh. Yeh, I've got it.

JOE

I've gone through more hell here in three days than I've had with Phyllis in three years.

TOMMY

(*Grimly rising*)

Phyllis? Who is Phyllis? Are you living with some other woman in Pittsburgh? You can't do this.

JOE

(*Springing to his feet*)

I'm not living with anybody! Phyllis is my secretary, and there's nothing between us!

TOMMY

Then why did you say you've been going through hell for three years?

JOE

(*Yelling*)

'Cause you get me all balled up!

(ELLEN *stomps downstairs with a suitcase and sets it down.*)

TOMMY

Here . . . here's your nail file. (*Hands it to her*) You didn't pack anything!

ELLEN

I've been packed for three days!

TOMMY

(*His voice threatens to break, but he holds out*)

Well, you can't go with just one suitcase. . . . There isn't much here, but—there're the books. They're yours. Most of them I gave to you. (*He turns away.*)

ELLEN

Can I have *The Shropshire Lad?* Isn't that the one that has: "And now the fancy passes by . . ."

TOMMY

"And nothing will remain. . . ." (*He brings her the book*

196

from the bookcase. Everyone is miserable. MICHAEL *sticks his head in the front door.)*

MICHAEL
(Beaming)

You've just five minutes to get to your class, Mr. Turner. We'll wait for you in the car. *(He goes out.)*

TOMMY
(Bravely)

Well, so long, Joe. I know you'll get her a place of her own for a while anyway. You can take that four-poster money with you, Ellen. I'll have one more check coming, too. *(He starts slowly upstairs.)*

JOE

What's "four-poster money"?

ELLEN
(Her voice trembling pathetically)

We were saving up to buy a new bed. *(She cries, and collapses on settee.)*

JOE

Oh, God, here we go again!

TOMMY
(Comes back again, desperately)

Why did you have to ask what four-poster money is? *(To* ELLEN*)* Ellen, please.

ELLEN
(Hysterically)

Oh, go on! Go on! Put on your coat. If you're going to be

197

kicked out of school, you can't go over there looking like a tramp.

TOMMY
(*Balefully*)
All right! (*He clumps upstairs like King Lear.*)

JOE
Look, Ellen, everything's gonna be all right.

ELLEN
Is it?

JOE
(*Looking after* TOMMY)
I wouldn't worry about that guy.

ELLEN
I don't!

JOE
I mean he's sure to get another job. He's had more publicity than Wally Myers.

ELLEN
I don't care what becomes of him. (JOE *studies her drooping figure narrowly.*)

JOE
Come here. (*He pulls her to her feet, facing him*) You're still crazy about that guy, aren't you?

ELLEN
I'm kind of scared of him. He used to be just—nice, but now he's wonderful!

(TOMMY *appears on stairs in time to catch the end of this. Very slowly light begins to dawn upon him.* JOE *sees him, but* ELLEN *doesn't.*)

JOE

I don't think he's so wonderful.

ELLEN

Yes, he is! That letter's wonderful. What he's trying to do is wonderful. He wouldn't let me or you or anyone stop him. Even Ed.

JOE

He's a scrapper, all right, but he can't dance. (*He crosses to the Victrola, pulling her along. He has an idea and does everything for* TOMMY's *benefit.* TOMMY *comes down slowly.* JOE *turns on the Victrola, which plays "Who?"*)

ELLEN

Oh, who wants to dance now?
(JOE *makes her dance, keeping her back to* TOMMY.)

JOE

This is important. It's all in the light you give off.

ELLEN

Light? What are you talking about?

JOE

(*With intensity*)

The important thing about dancing is that the man has

got to lead. (*He beckons to* TOMMY; *with one stride,* TOMMY *turns her away from* JOE.)

TOMMY

May I cut in?

ELLEN

Tommy! Let me go!

TOMMY
(*Shouting*)
No, I think you're wonderful, too!

ELLEN
You think I'm dumb! Were you listening?

TOMMY

No, I wasn't.

JOE
(*Up near door*)
Hey—don't start that again!

TOMMY
(*Puts on his hat, still dancing feverishly*)
Joe—why don't you go back to your wife? We can send her a wire.

JOE
Don't worry about me, brother. I sent her a wire this morn-

ing. (*He goes out into the fresh air, a happy man.* TOMMY *still dances with* ELLEN—*they are almost in tears.*)

TOMMY

Quit leading!

ELLEN

I'm not leading! You *were* listening!

TOMMY

You were yelling. Well, turn!

ELLEN

Make me turn. (*He does*) Don't be so rough—and put your hat on straight! You look terrible! (*Half-crying, she throws her arms around* TOMMY. *They are kissing each other very, very hard as the*

Curtain Falls

234

#294 4122